EXPLODING INTO LIFE

Exploding Into Life

DOROTHEA LYNCH · EUGENE RICHARDS

APERTURE IN ASSOCIATION WITH MANY VOICES PRESS

I am stunned.

Right under my fingers, as big as a wad of bubble gum, only harder, like the cap on the toothpaste tube. I feel it again, and my stomach jumps right up into my chest.

No. Through the apartment, touching the leaves of plants. No. Feed the cats. Open the refrigerator. Close the refrigerator. I can't eat. I can't read, can't watch anymore of a television movie about a meteor falling straight into downtown Phoenix, people screaming and glass flying, a foolish movie that leaves me gasping. I am thinking of that thing, buried in my breast, breathing and nesting and eating like a fleshy mouth. I call Dr. Dragonas. "But maybe I'm just being silly," I say. "I'm only thirty-four. I don't even smoke anymore."

I am supposed to cover a school committee for tomorrow's paper, but I just can't do it. I walk through the streets. It has begun to snow, sifting and hissing against the ground. I smell woodsmoke, someone's cozy fire. My father loved a fire, in all kinds of weather, but particularly in this kind of cold. Silver-haired, with his arm drawn back, snowball in hand, laughing—I have a photograph of him like that. His teeth were exactly like mine, very white and perfectly shaped. To share even the same mouth and nose and drooped left eyelid. Martha, my cousin, died of cancer last year at thirty-three. Twelve years ago, I danced with her brother Bill in a little café, just before he landed in Vietnam and was killed. I remember dancing close, because neither of us felt like cousins, and laughing, and the lights turning blue with cigarette smoke.

6

I sit on the edge of the examining table while Dr. Dragonas probes and tests. I would like to rest my head against his shoulder. Pressure against my left breast stirs the ache again, so like a toothache. In his waiting room I had felt diseased, a carrier among the pregnant women with their different-sized stomachs. I am young enough to be having my first child. Dr. Dragonas discovers a second lump up high in my armpit that has been aching for the last few days like a strained muscle.

What is it? What is it? But he will give nothing away except a shot of Metaxa brandy that he keeps for emergencies. He and the nurse with curly blonde hair take turns calling hospitals, looking for a bed and an operating room.

"Breast resection," they say into the beige telephones.

Resection. It sounds like refashion, as if they are going to remake my breast. No one says the word "malignant," or "tumor," or "cancer."

"We'll just put you into the hospital for a few days and take a sampling of those tissues to find out what's going on," Dr. Dragonas says. "Don't worry, Dorothea, it's just a biopsy."

Perhaps, I am already crying when I get on the elevator in the parking garage, for the man standing next to me looks at my face and then down at his shoes. Rain has begun, and it is bitterly cold. Gene is in New York, photographing. I call my newspaper to tell them I cannot go to work. I need to talk to someone, so I drive to my mother's house. Up until I was fourteen, I always thought of it as my father's house. It was my father who defined the boundaries of my life: *his* pear tree, *his* two peach trees, *his* narrow white house with black shutters on a dead end street in Dorchester, Massachusetts. There was my mother and my older sister Moira and my little brother Billy, of course, but my father was the one. He died in his sleep when I was fourteen.

I stand in the middle of her living room, still wearing my coat, and my mother stares at me without speaking. Ill with liver disease, her body is swollen and yellow. She is frightened by my tears. The TV blares in the corner because my mother is deaf—*The Odd Couple*—I am interrupting her favorite program. When it ends, Oscar and Felix are still friends, and I am drunk from a highball my brother has given me.

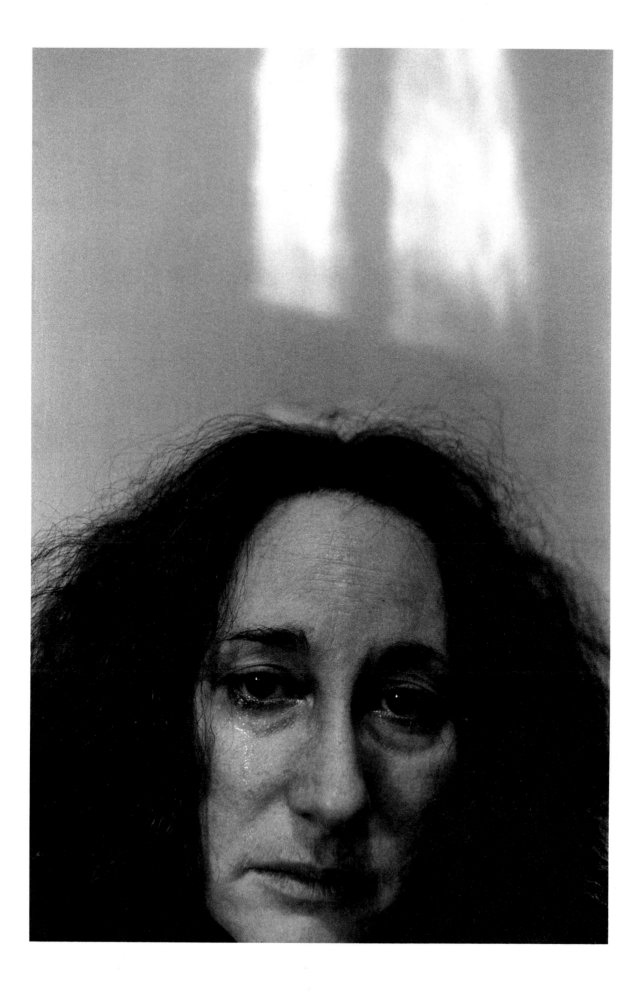

Back at my own apartment I walk from room to room trying to get myself under control. My cats and plants and books are no protection against the circling black cloud. One aunt, three cousins, four uncles—all of them dead or dying from cancer. But writing the names of the people I love makes me feel better. I sit at my typewriter and make a will, leaving my silver ring and car to Gene; crystal beads to my mother; shell necklace to Tessie, Gene's mother; and an Indian silver bird charm to my friend Eileen, who doesn't own many things.

So there is something worse, after all, than your man turning away from you. Your own body turning away, running away with a crazy new life of its own.

The afternoon light is piercing white. Snow color. The wind is like a blow to our faces. Shivering from nervousness and the cold, I kiss Gene's parents good-bye and slide into the car. Good-bye, good-bye.

Gene smiles at me. "Don't cry," he says. "One would think you're going on a long, long trip."

"Well, I am," I answer in surprise, not being clever at all. "Aren't I?"

Blood sample, lung capacity test for the anesthesiologist, electrocardiogram, x-rays. A man in a lab coat pulls the chest x-rays out of an apparatus that looks like a Coke machine. Checking the names written on them, he turns and looks at me in my voluminous hospital wrapper, then down at the x-rays again. Is that mine, I want to ask. Can you tell me if the lumps show?

Pale-faced and worried women in bathrobes walk up and down, up and down in the ward. Shuffling and bent, up, then back again. "What are you here for?" several of them call over to me, friendly and nosey at once. "What are you here for?" They are like a Greek chorus. Harpies. "What are you here for? Have you had yours yet?"

Dorothy across the ward is having her hernia examined by her doctor. "Don't you ever wear mittens?" she asks him. "Your hands are so cold."

The nurse shaves the hairs around my breast. "The doctor wouldn't be able to see a thing otherwise," Irene says smiling at me. "They wear those magnifiers doing a biopsy, you know, and it would look like a forest." She nicks me a few times, shaving off small moles.

"Would you mind if I felt the area?"

She presses firmly, running her fingers into my armpit where the larger lump aches all by itself. "I've felt a lot of breast lumps in my life," she says, "and I don't think you have anything to worry about. Aren't you only thirty-four? Well, then . . ."

The lump is so small I wouldn't have noticed it if Gene hadn't touched me, stroking and kissing in our warm Sunday afternoon bed. A bruise, I thought. A pulled muscle. My period. The next morning my hand found the same soreness and beneath the soreness, the lump.

Irene turns out all the lights. The snow falls against the hospital walls, and around me the women breathe like tired animals. The hospital rocks a little in the wind, groans, a large ship getting underway.

At 7:30 a.m. a nursing attendant rolls white elastic stockings up my legs, squeezing my cold feet gently with her warm hands, then wheels me down the hospital corridor to the operating room. The walls slide by. Gonzo. I am really Gonzo on their Demerol, head rocking around. Faces in masks, flowered caps. "Are you Dorothea? . . . Hello, are you Dorothea? . . . Are you Dorothea Lynch?" And then nothing at all. Blackness. I try to lift my eyelids, one eyelid. Nothing moves. I must be dead.

What is this? What is this pain? Ferocious, tearing open my armpit. I can hear their voices. How can I be dead? I try to wiggle my foot, my finger. Then. It's the doctor making the pain. Dragonas saying, "Oh, oh. This doesn't look so good."

When I open my eyes it is nighttime, and Gene is alone by the side of my bed. No results? No results. I try to tell him what I think I heard during the biopsy, but I am too tired.

When I open my eyes Gene is with my mother and some of my friends. My mother is reading aloud from a children's book, and everyone is laughing. I cannot understand any of it. What has happened? But my mother reads on and on.

When I open my eyes again, Dr. Dragonas comes in wearing his overcoat, bringing in the cold night air as he unwraps a red plaid scarf from his neck.

"Well, Dorothea," he says, standing beside my bed, "you do have the disease."

Malignant. I awaken in the morning in a fog of medication with the word malignant on my tongue. I say it aloud, though the nurse who gives me a shot for pain will not talk about the biopsy. Dr. Dragonas arrives to change the surgical dressings and tells me they had to cut my left breast to sample the tumor. The cut on the right breast, a mirror image biopsy, was done because some breast cancer patients have a tumor in their other breast.

But I don't really understand much of what he is saying. "Three out of four lymph nodes involved . . . a bone scan to survey metastatic sites . . . then we will plan your protocol." I put my hands over my face until the nurses come in to move me downstairs. The day passes in a blur of sleep.

Before dawn a large man in a navy blue, three-piece suit wakes me. In a voice so casual and so precise he could be talking about school budgets, Dr. Robert Shirley explains that a modified radical mastectomy means removal of my left breast and the lymph glands under my arm. Or, I might choose to have primary radiation therapy instead—long needles with radium implants stuck into my breast. "Maybe not the best thing," says Dr. Shirley, "what with the possible radiation spray effects that could generate tumor activity in the other breast."

A radiologist, Dr. Kinsella, visits my room next to tell me about this very same primary radiation therapy. Dr. Kinsella doesn't know what Dr. Shirley, a surgical oncologist, means by a "spraying effect." Not in his experience, he says, has it ever happened. "We would give you twenty-five external radiation treatments, but we would use radiation shields to protect the rest of the body. The implant is a fairly low dosage and only remains in place for a few days."

I look at the doctors and I think of undertakers, straight and dark and inescapable. "Interstitial implant, morbidity, adjunctive chemotherapy." Listening to them is like trying to decipher the code in my Graham Greene spy stories where finding the answer means saving the hero's life. "Of course, it's your decision after all," each doctor tells me. "Radiation or surgery. You decide."

On the green TV screen above my head, I see my femur, my pelvis, even my liver, outlined by radioactivity, all looking like sparkling constellations. I have been injected with "tracer material" and am lying on a hard table that moves up and

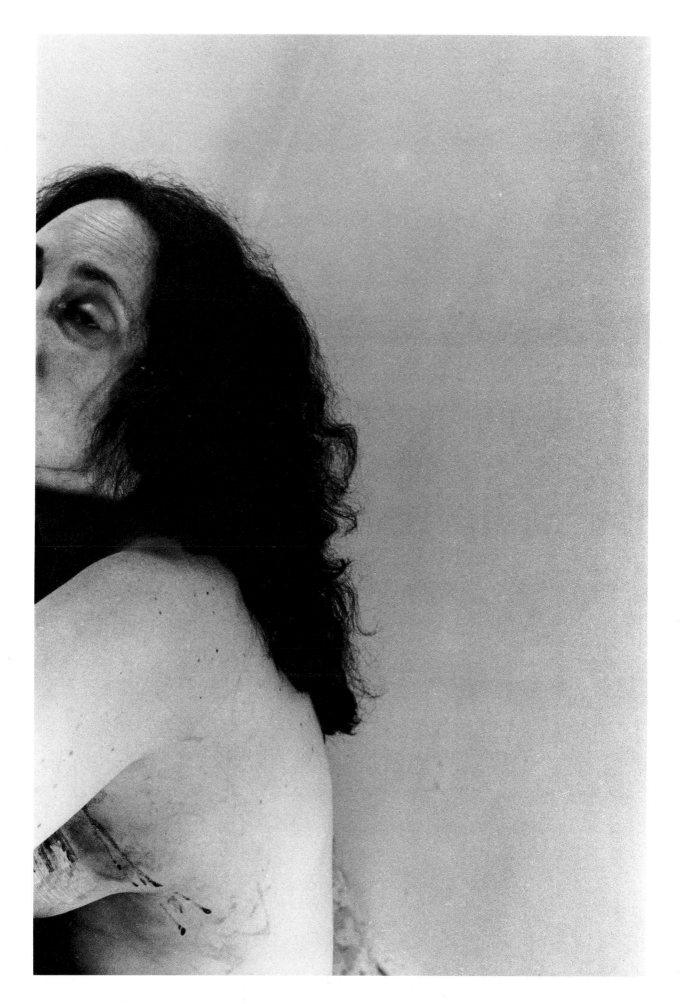

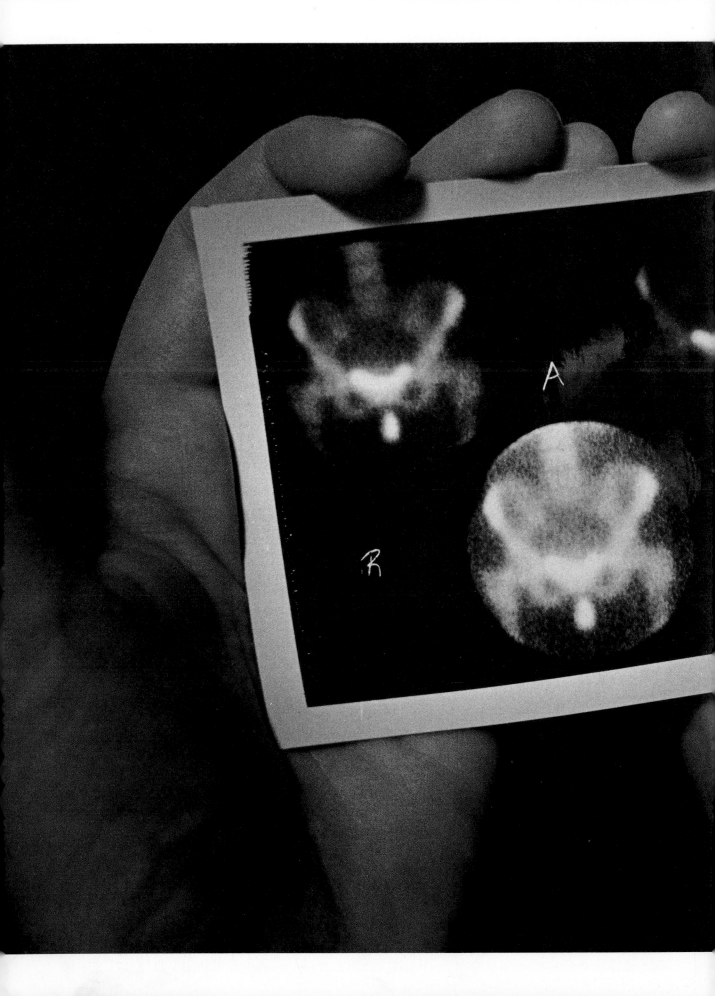

down and sideways and makes little clicking sounds each time a picture is taken. This bone scan is a search for additional tumors, cancer seedlings, that may already have slipped like invaders from my breast to my lymph glands and into my blood.

After an hour a small Japanese doctor appears next to me, beaming and clapping his hands together. "Clear. Clear," he says. "One hundred percent."

My hands are shaking, and I try to catch my lower lip between my teeth to stop it from quivering. I have no idea what he means.

"Good news," the nurse says, squeezing my hands.

Good news. There are no distant mestastases. The cancer is still in my breast, but it has not yet spread anywhere else. A little cancer, not a lot. I think they are telling me I am not dying.

When I tell Gene the results of the bone scan, he puts up a hand to hide his shiny, pink-rimmed eyes from me. I've been taking his stoicism for granted. We have been best friends, lovers for fifteen years; yet I never remember him crying like this.

Dr. Dragonas finds us with our arms around each other, heads together, crying and laughing at the same time. The doctor is ready to discharge me. He tells me how to change the dressings over the biopsy wound when I get home, but he is a little curt, annoyed that I have made no treatment decision.

Radiation or surgery? I am like the character in the children's fable; behind which door hides the tiger, which door the lady? Dr. Dragonas draws himself up, looking for all the world like an inflexible old world Papa. "By all means," he says, "go ahead and take a look at the options. But don't wait too long!"

I try to find out what a mastectomy looks like so I call the American Cancer Society. The woman on the other end tells me that books with pictures of cancer treatments aren't considered suitable for non-medical people. Volunteers at the National Cancer Institute and Cancer Information Service refuse to discuss primary radiation or other alternatives to surgery, instead counseling me to have a mastectomy, the "proven method of treatment."

I tell my friends all that's been happening to me and I ask them what they think I should do.

"You should look for books that will help you decide . . ."

"I don't think you should rush into anything. There's a doctor in Texas or California, somewhere out West, who is treating breast cancer patients with vitamins. We would have done that with my mother if there had been time . . ."

"Do you know you don't have to get a mastectomy anymore? What about just having a lumpectomy?"

"If it were me, I would have radiation instead of surgery."

Rain, rain. Gene and I spend a cold, wet afternoon searching through bookstores in Harvard Square. Muzak jingles ring over and over; people are shopping for Christmas gifts. We find a book about cancer treatment from which I learn something about chemotherapy, but there are no pictures to show me what a woman with one breast looks like. On the shelves are books of a senile old man dying of starvation, young children with distended bellies crying with hunger, men and women blown apart by bombs.

At home I pore over photographs Gene has made of me: happy family snapshots, fifteen-year-old prom pictures from the days we first began dating, blue nudes, sunset nudes. "Make a picture of me now," I tell him. If he takes a photograph today, it will show the bloody scars from the biopsy. Until a few days ago, I didn't know what one looked like. And there must be thousands of women who undergo the slice-and-snip-and-examine procedure without knowing the first thing about it.

We women, how in the dark we are about our bodies and what can happen to them. We ask in whispers, in the corner at a party or on the telephone, what does a breast lump feel like? What does cancer look like? Will I be all right?

Gene sits me on one of the mattresses on the bedroom floor. The room is cold. The sun, setting behind the house next door, leaves one bar of light high on the wall. He makes the photograph.

All I want to do is climb into bed with the cats and sleep. I wish someone else would visit doctors, look for books, make the right decision. But Gene is like a mosquito, needling, pushing, telling me to get up, get dressed.

He brings me to Dr. Peter Deckers a surgical oncologist at University Hospital to get a second opinion. Dr. Deckers is a huge man with ruffled hair and rumpled clothes. He lightly touches my biopsy wound, and then he sits, stooped a little, reading the pathology reports I have brought along. He agrees with the findings sent over from Boston Hospital for Women.

"If you were my wife, I would tell you to have surgery. And yes, I would follow it up with chemotherapy as added insurance."

Up until now, I have known Dr. Deckers only as the doctor of Ruth Jacome, a family friend. "Poor Ruthie," everyone called her, after her cigarette cough was diagnosed as advanced lung cancer. Day after day, relatives would telephone progress reports to those of us who didn't have the courage to visit Ruth: "Ruthie got up out of bed today; Ruthie went for a ride to the ocean today; today Ruth is sitting outside in the sun."

On the evening of Ruth's funeral, a photography exhibit opened at a small gallery run by Gene and his friends. "Death's Final Privacy" was the title of the show, and among the pictures of mourning and funerals were poems by T. S. Eliot and Walt Whitman and a children's nursery rhyme: "The worms crawl in, the worms crawl out, the worms play pinochle on your snout, your stomach turns a slimy green, and pus pours out like thick whipped cream."

To the Victoria Diner, our old haunt in Dorchester, for brandy alexanders, sweet boozy milkshakes. In back where it is dark and the waitresses don't bother you, we hold hands and talk about living long enough to do the things we want to do.

When I was a child, I thought I would become a great poet. What I wanted was a bohemian life like Edna St. Vincent Millay, but I didn't even leave home until I was twenty-five to write poetry at graduate school in Indiana. My best poem that year was "The Abandoned House":

> . . . *as if tree-*
> *tied cowbirds or the tap-tap-tap of sun—*
> *struck snow upon the roof could set me free.*
> *Not free*
> *perhaps, only*
> *loosened like a seed pod in wind-torn fields*
> *waiting for the sun to crack me wide, while*
> *the grass stands up around me like a shield.*

I stand in front of the bedroom mirror and hold my hand over my left breast covering the nipple. I try to imagine what it would look like. "What are you doing?" Gene asks.

I decide to go ahead with surgery. Treatments with radiation would mean sitting beneath an x-ray machine day after day, waiting for the tumor to shrink, dry up, die. It seems the way to get rid of this cancer is to cut it out from my body. I want to get rid of it quick, quick.

Tonight I cannot sleep. I am obsessed with when that one different voracious cell in my breast first exploded into life. The books say tumors can grow for years before they are detectible to the touch. So I can't help wondering if it was already in place that night we skinny-dipped at Sunset Lake, or when I covered my first news story, or that summer I spent trying to run more than a mile.

Gene lies beside me, restless, wanting sex. How could anyone be attracted to me right now, with my oozing, discolored breasts and my frozen thoughts? I wish I could explain to him that it isn't just the loss of a breast that's troubling me. It is what the loss symbolizes, a premonition of the day when all the cells in my body are extinguished like cold stars.

"Maybe you should make photographs of the whole thing," I tell Gene. "If there aren't any pictures of mastectomies, maybe you should take pictures of mine."

"No," Gene says looking upset. "No, I couldn't. We have no permission to photograph inside the hospital. And a camera would be in the way when I'm with you."

"Come on," I bully him. "You're always criticizing me and our friends for not recording the important events in our lives."

Permission forms: one for the anesthetist; one for Boston Hospital for Women; one for the doctor; and, of course, one for the lab. The old phrase, signing your life away, comes to my mind, but I do not say it aloud. Then I'm led down the hospital corridor, hung with cardboard Christmas trees and colored wreaths, to a tiny white room with a midget television.

Gene is waiting in a chair by the window, his camera around his neck. The room turns bluer, darker. Twilight. We sit without speaking, as if tomorrow morning's operation will never happen.

Dr. Shirley, now in charge of my treatment, is surprised when we tell him we want to make photographs, to try and salvage something from this experience. I hold my breath, afraid he will be cynical or abrupt, but he says, "Sure. What you do in this room is your own business." Dr. Shirley, who looks like an aging, pink-cheeked football player, seems pleased with himself. For the first time in weeks, I am happier, feeling more in control.

With his finger, Dr. Shirley demonstrates tomorrow morning's incision. "We will go up to the clavicle and make the incision down to the chest wall. The whole breast peels off rather nicely," he says. An incision in the shape of a smiling mouth. They will clean off the lymph nodes, the chest wall, the arm muscles, and my long, splendid ropes of veins.

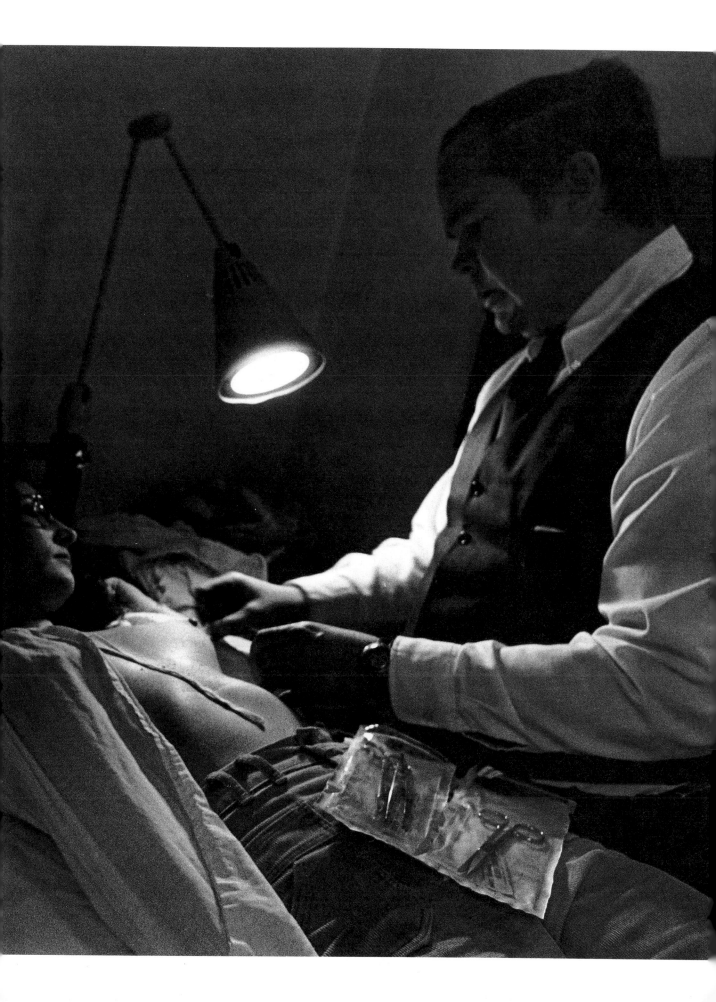

My mother and brother visit my room after supper. My mother is flustered, smelling as if she has been drinking. My brother is gray-skinned from a car accident two days ago that has left him with a concussion. For some reason, they have brought along one of my brother's friends, whom I do not know, and they all stand awkwardly around my bed. "Too many people," the nurses complain. My brother makes small talk, and my mother dozes in her chair. I wish they would leave so I could spend some time alone with Gene.

My brother hands me a gift, a gold chain and his own St. Christopher medal. St. Christopher, the patron saint of travelers. It is such an innocent gift, it makes me ashamed of my impatience and anger with them, and I blink to get rid of the tears.

The medicine cart is on its way. Visiting hours are over. My brother looks lost, still unable to say anything, so I give him "thumbs-up" and a smile.

The young nurse, who comes to shave my underarm and chest, tells me not to worry. "You'll be all right," she says, her face next to mine. "Look at Happy Rockefeller. She lost both her breasts."

Gerry Butler, a stout, black nurse, moves in like a heavy cloud. I have been asking her to bring me a sleeping pill since 10:30, and it is now past midnight. Finally, she brings it along with a cup of water, goes away, and comes back again asking, "Did you say your prayers?"

"Prayers! Who the hell do you think you are anyway?" I want to yell, "This is my business." But I say nothing, just watch her move towards me. Shaking her head and sighing she takes my hand, palm up, and closes her own over it. My bed is raised close to her face.

"Take care of our sister, Lord," she says. "She will be in your hands. We do not ask that you take this burden from her. Rather, we ask for your help to bear the burden. We never ask for you to remove the pain, Lord, but help our sister be strong. Help her boyfriend, and let him know, as well as our sister, that beauty and love do not originate in the body, but in the love between two people. Help her friends and family to support her and love her in this time when she needs them."

I lean over to kiss her cheek, unable to say anything, not even thank you.

I am exhausted, and there is a silence around me, but I can't sleep yet—I won't let myself slip over the edge. Gene. I keep thinking of him, that straight gaze, saying few words, the enclosing arm at the right time.

Seems impossible that I've known him since I was eighteen. We were both freshmen at Northeastern University in Boston. Having come out of a little Catholic

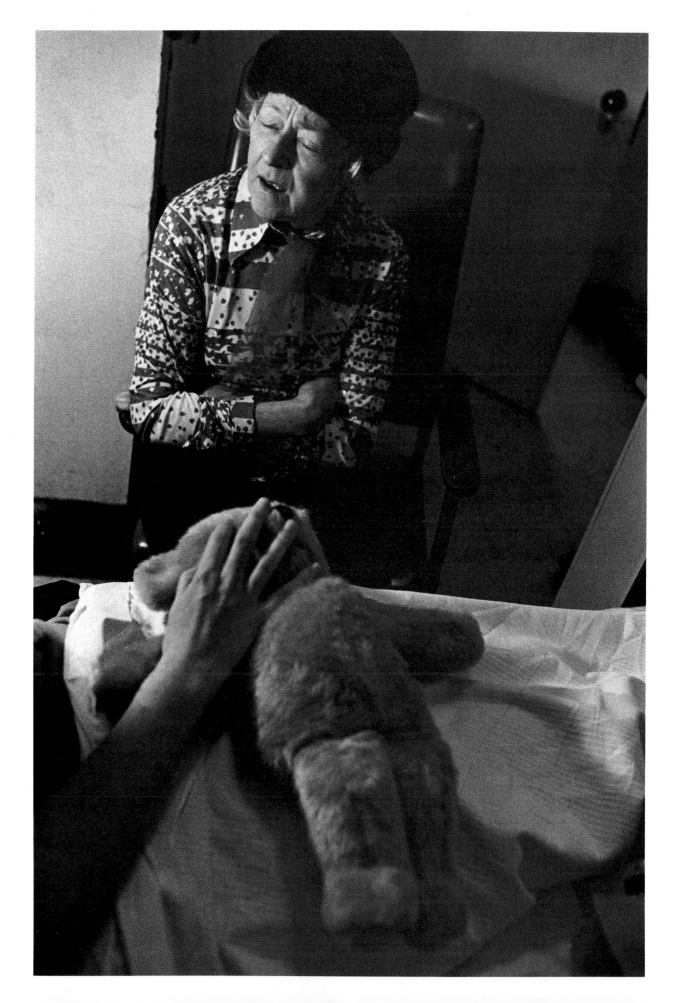

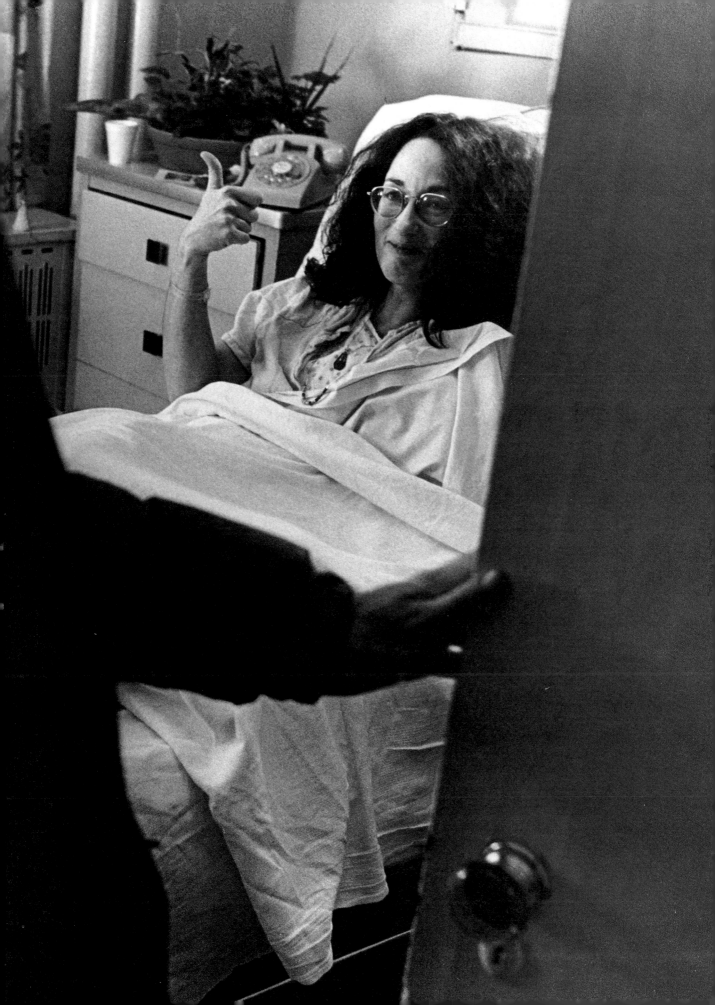

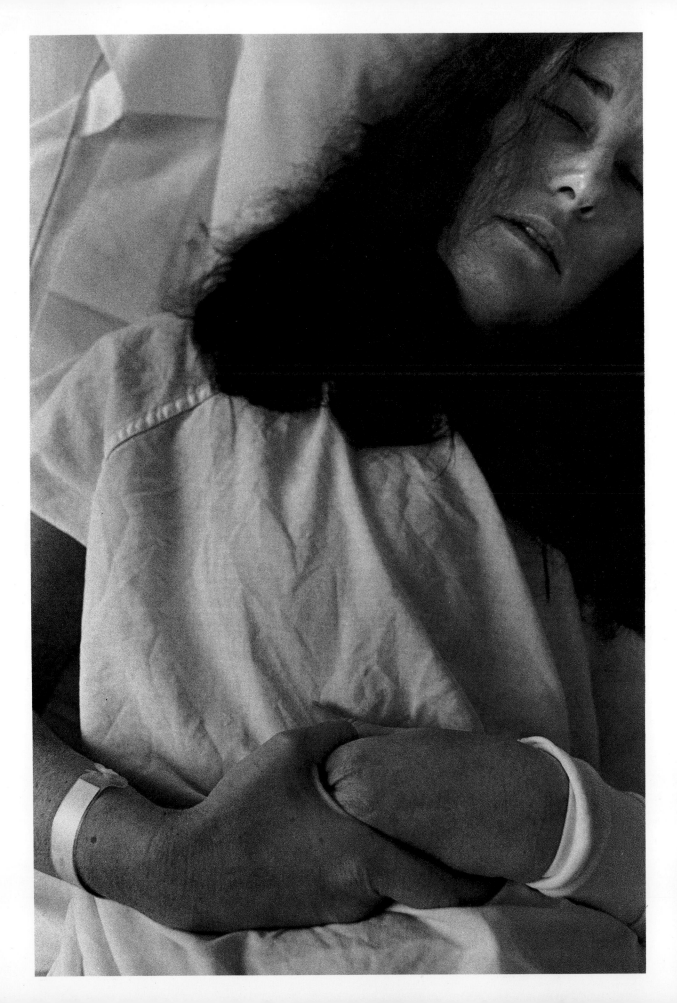

academy with a scholarship—it was the nuns who convinced me to be a writer—I was aware of my schoolgirl status. Gene was "academically non-prestigious" his energy raw and undirected. I wrote poetry; he did not read poetry. I read novels; he read the front pages of newspapers and every magazine that hit the stands. He was rebellious, overheated, a draft resister.

Ours was a terrible, wonderful clash of minds, but that was sixteen years ago, and so much has superseded it. I can't remember much right now, except the powerful sexual attraction I felt for him, with his sensuous mouth and fierce blue eyes. Oh, he was beautiful.

"Don't you want to get up and use the toilet?" a nurse whispers. "You can brush your teeth, but don't swallow any water. This shot will dry out your mouth but make you more relaxed."

I was warm and calm when I woke, but now the fear returns coating my tongue with a hot, metallic taste. My heart is chattering away inside my chest. Perhaps, I will die of a heart attack before they have a chance to cut me open.

"Can you climb onto the cart yourself, Dorothea?" How can I climb? I am so dizzy. I feel sick. "What? Are you going to be sick? She can't be sick. There's nothing in her stomach. Do you feel sick, Dorothea? Are you Dorothea? Are you Dorothea Lynch?" Everyone is in masks. There are Dr. Shirley and Dr. Dragonas. "This is just going to make you go to sleep."

Sunlight and pain, sunlight and voices. The sting of needles, hands forcing me to roll from one side to another, cough, cough again. Bandages tight across the chest, great engulfing fog, pain sharp in my arm; but someone arranges the pillow perfectly, precisely, so the pain can flow away. "Cough, can you cough, Dorothea?"

A nurse, minutes, maybe hours later, props a tray over my belly, then lifts me up onto the pillow and puts a spoon in my hand. I watch her peel a soft-boiled egg and mash it.

"Eat, eat," she says.

I would like to tell her I don't like soft-boiled eggs, but I am too tired, and the spoon feels good in my hand. So solid. Real. Yolk sticks to it and to my teeth.

Dragonas and Dr. Shirley arrive together, faces shiny from shaving. They tell me they have been in conference. Dragonas is shy, apologetic, and smiling too much, as

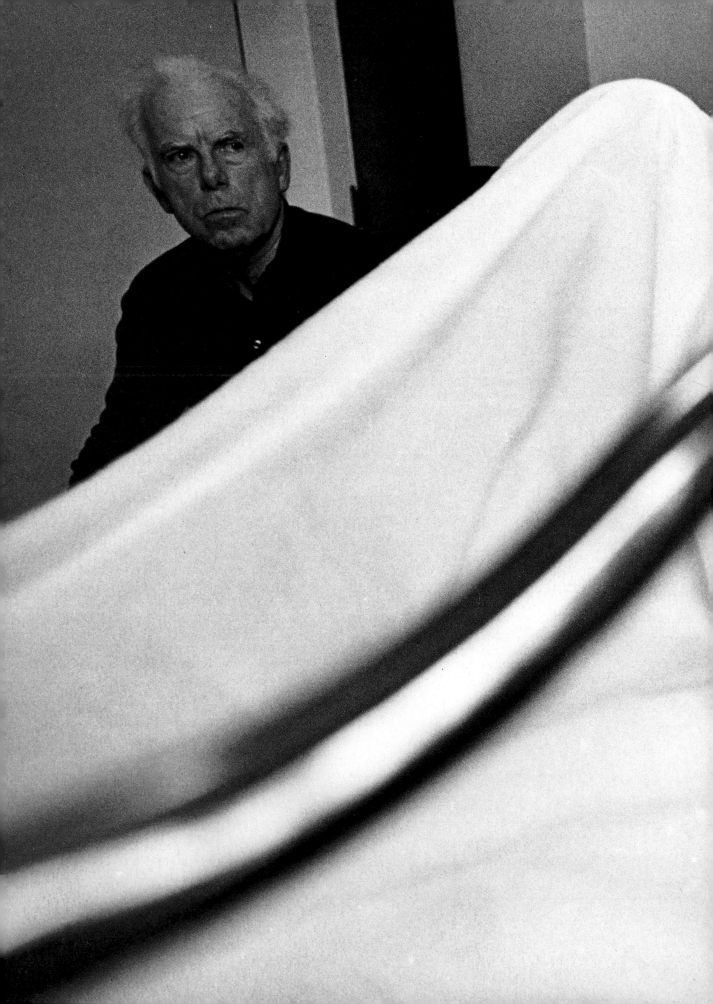

if he has committed some unforgiveable act. He sips from a container of coffee while Shirley unwraps my bandages.

"Look at it, Dorothea," they tell me, raising me up.

"No. No." I tell them I can't see without my glasses.

Deep breath. I look down at the purple black line, an eight-inch-long, puckered and black-stitched cut. There is a drainage tube stuck in a hole in my side. It is kept from falling inside my body by a safety pin. The breast remaining is a surprise, its nipple as pink as a girl's pout. Where I had expected a gaping hole and raw flesh, there is a little skin remaining—their attempt to leave as much as possible. Clean, necessary.

In the ward on the top floor of the old hospital, I am the only patient, except for a girl who talks all morning long. I hear her through my curtains, when the nurses draw them around the bed, and through my closed eyelids. All afternoon I drift in and out of sleep. I am dreaming some silly dream. A woman carrying a clipboard says she is doing a research project on cancer patients and asks if I smoke cigarettes, drink, eat meat, have ever taken the pill, or had x-rays. Gene argues with the head nurse who blocks the camera when he tries to make a picture of me in bed having my hair combed. "You can't take pictures in here. I don't care what Dr. Shirley says. The hospital is the one to give permission."

In and out of sleep. Gene by the window.

"I'm your night nurse," Mrs. Carr says. She is like a chill wind, a thin, tight face set into a scowl. She rolls me onto my side. Her fingers are cold against my back as she unwinds the gauze. She makes little retching sounds in her throat. The bloody discharge is sticky against my skin, and I am embarrassed.

"The ones I really mind are the advanced cases," Mrs. Carr says. "Open sores that are draining. Those are contagious, and I don't like to touch them."

"She's a real bitch," complains my roommate. "The other night I was in the bathroom throwing up, I couldn't even get up off the floor, and she wouldn't help me. I don't know what's the matter with her."

Mrs. Carr measures my fluid intake against my urine amounts, and she brings in blow-bottles to exercise my anesthesia-laden lungs. But most of the time she stands in one corner of the ward, arms wrapped around herself, watching me like a predator—Poe's night raven.

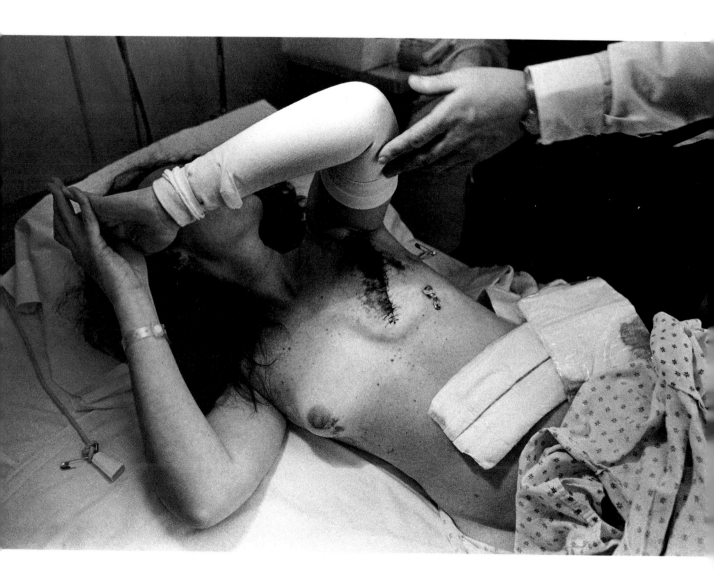

34

"I don't want any more pain medicine," I tell her. "I'm not in any pain."

It is not the truth. I can sense her disgust with me. She makes me feel synonymous with my disease, loathesome. I am afraid she will give me the wrong medicine or an incorrect dosage. "Or something poisonous," says a voice in the back of my head.

"Your physician has left the order for you to have a shot for pain," she says, holding the syringe casually in one hand. "I really think you should have a shot."

"No, I don't want it."

I am sure she will feel my fright when she places her cool fingers on my pulse. The needle slides painlessly into the skin near my hip.

"See?" she says briskly. "It doesn't hurt at all."

Gene has arranged for me to be transferred to another floor, away from Mrs. Carr. I have a tiny, white room all to myself, new sheets beneath my legs. I lie perfectly still, at last feeling quiet inside my body. Outside my window birds call, starling and sparrow, and there is a dazzle of sun from Jamaica Pond. I have not watched the changing light of a whole afternoon for a long, long time.

From my bed I see a frail, jaundice-colored woman make her way up and down the corridor several times a day. Shuffle, shuffle, stop. Shuffle, shuffle, stop. She pushes an intravenous pole that carries plastic bags of yellow and brown liquids, all of them connected to her by long plastic hoses. I call out hello, and invite her into my room. Her name is Gertie Phillips. I cannot tell her age; her skin hangs in folds, and her eyes are deeply shadowed.

Gertie tells me she has had a stomach tumor removed. She mispronounces words like "ileostomy" and "colostomy," and never says the word "cancer". "The bags don't fit very well," she says. "They leak, and then the nurses have to help me." She does not want to stain the white lambswool coverlet on her bed that protects against bedsores.

"What would you think about this?" Gertie asks Gene, when he visits her room one afternoon. She lifts her hospital gown, so he can see the clean, rounded holes in her side from which the plastic hoses coil. "Would that make you sick?" Gertie is concerned that the bags filled with wastes will disgust her husband.

Gene explains that one of his friends, Tom Fitzgerald, who almost died from colitis, now wears a bag at his waist. Tom felt like such a freak after his ileostomy, Gene tells her, that he left his home and wife and schoolwork to join the Ringling Brothers Circus. But after six months he came home, feeling stronger, ready to start up his life again.

Gertie means a lot to me, that tiny, white figure struggling up and down the corridor, a little farther each day.

It is the week before Christmas. I have been in the hospital for four days. Gene brings me a tiny Christmas tree with red, blue, and green birds to clip to the branches. My other friends come, too: Joyce, Tom and Roswell, Hollysue, Eileen, Eleanor, and Kevin. I love them for caring, but they are so frightened and jubilant and tender-skinned, they exhaust me—eight of them visiting at once, packed against the wall, smiling and holding me with their eyes, as if I were a holy relic of some kind, a new strange form of life.

A lady with blonde hair pokes her head into my room, calling cheerfully, "Hello there, Dorothea. Are you keeping busy? Want me to send the crafts cart along for something to do? What are you writing?" I have no idea who she is. Someone is always walking into my hospital room, acting as if we have already met, old friends and all that. It is the medical professional's way of attempting to put a patient at ease. But it is disconcerting to me not to know to whom I am talking.

The woman eventually introduces herself as Helen. She's a psychologist. I show her my notebooks, explaining that I am writing about what it is like to have cancer. Why? Because writing is what I do. It helps me sort out ideas and emotions and find out what I really feel.

Slowly, deliberately, Helen nods her head, not saying a word. I want her approval, so I keep talking. Surely having cancer is as important as having a baby, or getting married, or sleeping with a man. Women write about those experiences all the time. I speak excitedly of the people who will help me—Dr. Dragonas, Dr. Shirley, the nurses here. I will ask hospitals to let me talk to cancer patients like Gertie.

The hospital psychiatrist, Dr. Gates, makes me nervous when he visits later in the day, constantly jotting notes on a pad. He is conducting an independent study on the psychological reactions of breast cancer patients. Answering his questions I am aware of sounding like a Pollyanna. What I mean to say twists away from me.

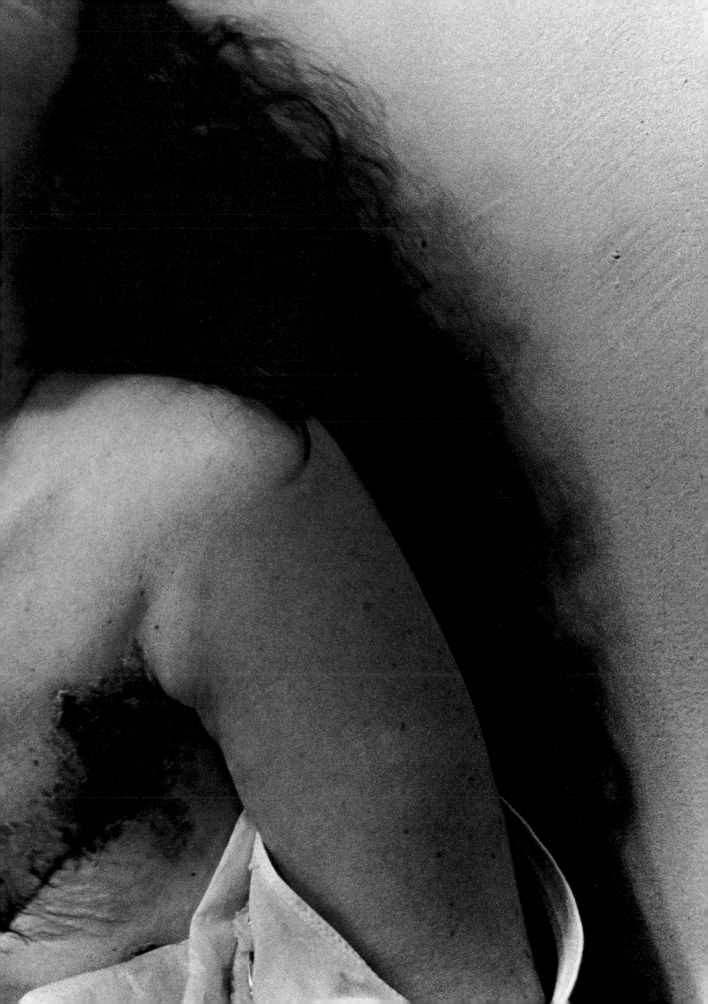

"Nothing is what I thought it would be," I tell him. "Not cancer, not dying, not being alive. I feel I've been given a reprieve, like lucky Lazaras, and have returned from the grave. The sound of my own heart is a miracle. The feel of clean sheets against my skin a . . ."

Dr. Gates interrupts to say I am experiencing a medical phenomenon called "euphoria," quite common after a major operation. What I should expect, he says, is to have sexual difficulties, be shorter-tempered and more impatient with people.

After Dr. Gates leaves I close the door and do twenty-five sit-ups and leg raises, careful not to crush my swollen arm, working against being a textbook cancer patient, I suppose. I keep wishing he would come back and catch me at it. Ah, one—two—three.

Sarah, the lady from the medical fitters, goes through her hat boxes pulling out bits of rubber, silicone, and cloth. She does not speak about cancer or surgery, and I wonder if her job of fitting breast cancer patients with fake tits is as normal and acceptable to her as it appears. Day after day of ravaged bodies, abnormalities, blood, stitches, draining wounds. She chats about sizes, letting me heft different models, little bags of mushy plastic that grow warm from the heat of my hand. Impossible not to remember the warm masculine palms that cradled my own breasts.

Gene is in the corner, his camera in front of his face, so I cannot tell what he is thinking. I feel silly surrounded by mirrors and the pink-and-white rubber mounds.

Prosthesis. I used to think it was a word for something dirty when I was in grammar school. My friends and I puzzled over the ads for false breasts hidden in the back pages of the movie magazines, giggling over the Frederick of Hollywood starlets in their see-through babydolls and pointy bras. Sarah places a prosthesis over my bandages so I can see "how natural it looks." It's hard for me to get excited about a wad of fiber, but I look into her mirror, nodding and smiling. I really wish she would go away. I am not sad or angry, but this whole procedure seems no more significant than selecting a pair of slippers. All I am doing is making myself more acceptable to polite society.

Hospital life is suspended life, blank stretches of time broken by the sounds going past my door: doctors' heavy tread; nurses' swift, tapping heels; the rattling food cart at 7:30, 11:30, 4:30; stretchers, clattering and tinny when no one is being carried, creaking when a gray-faced patient is aboard.

But the nights are different. I like the nights after all the visitors have gone. Nurses and patients are like girls at a pajama party, chatting freely, laughing, exchanging life stories. Last night Santa Claus came after visiting hours, accompanied by a clown and an invisible dog. The performers kissed the patients and told jokes until the sickest of us was laughing.

And hospital nights are mysterious, the corridors darkened so only the exit sign glows, the breath of a dozen strangers spilling into the air. I walk down the short hall unobserved and look through the operating room doors. This is the heart of the whole place, all neutral green and shining metal, with empty stretchers in a line. There is no sign of blood or flesh, no respirator or beeping heart monitor, no sign at all of my own journey through those doors.

The thrashing of tree limbs and a sound like a scream. He is just outside my window under the trees, hidden in the dark, the man with the red, glowing eyes. He circles around and around the wings of the hospital, darker than the darkness, looking for a way in. I am afraid to make any noise, afraid to turn in the narrow hospital bed. Afraid he has gotten inside after all, through an unlocked door, that he is standing and listening to the rustle of my sheets.

It is the wind that frightens me, that makes the hospital into an unsafe place, a storm, blowing in from the north, clearing up the clouds, and pushing them out to sea. It is the wind that wakes me. I put on the lamp beside my bed, wishing I were not too embarrassed to ring for Elyssa, the night nurse, to say, "Come sit with me, because I have had a nightmare." I know the man in the darkness is only a dream, but it is a dream that has brought the outside world with all its danger into this precisely ordered place.

I go out into the empty corridor, grateful for the glow of the lamp at the nurses' station. Someone calls out to me as I pass a doorway. It is Gertie, lying in the

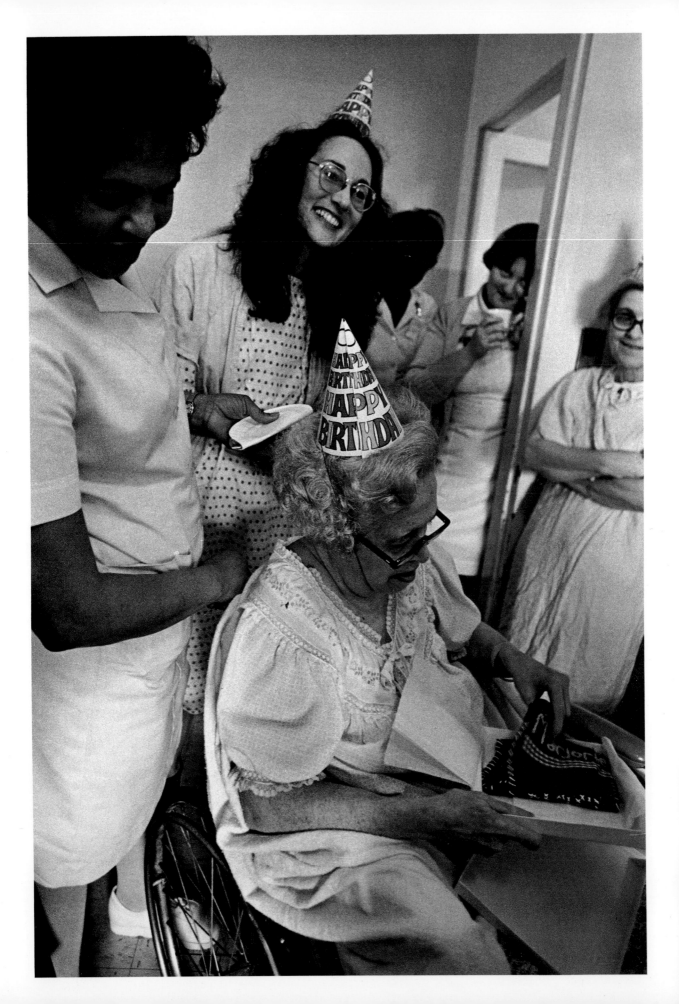

darkness, the whites of her eyes glowing. "Oh, I'm so glad to see you," she says. "I just had a terrible nightmare. I couldn't move; I was scared."

I tell her about my own nightmare, and she pats my hand to comfort me and tells me stories about her little dog and her husband back home. We kiss goodnight, and I go to my own bed, safe again. This is a new experience—to care for Gertie; and for the woman with lung cancer down the hall; and for the night nurse, Elyssa; for Dr. Shirley; even for crochety Marjorie, who just celebrated a birthday and is destined to spend the rest of her Christmases in a nursing home. Though Dr. Shirley talks about my going home for Christmas, I can't imagine being anyplace but here.

"Look at that sun, Gertie!" I say, watching the sun rise and the light spread along the underside of the clouds. We are all up early, too early. No one has slept well because today we are all going home, home for Christmas.

"That sun is the prettiest thing," Gertie calls across the row of bathroom sinks. "And it's good for you to see it. Life is beautiful."

I suppose we sound like two old farts. But it is difficult to contain our elation, so we are reduced to platitudes. I remember my father after his first heart attack and how he walked through the cool May mornings as if they were a gift. Standing outside in a pair of shorts, coffee cup in hand, he would listen to the birds, examining the trees for signs of nests or squirrels. "Ah," he would exclaim, slapping one hand against his bare belly, "what a great morning to be alive!"

I am the last patient on the floor to be discharged. The aides are waiting to strip my bed and dust the room. Gene, too, has been waiting, silent, for hours. He makes me nervous. There doesn't seem to be anything to say.

Finally, at noontime, Dr. Shirley barges in, apologizing for a baby who took hours to deliver. I hardly listen as he talks about bandages and doing my arm exercises and taking vitamin pills. "Good-bye," he says, and I am startled. It is really time to go home.

TWO

Biopsy: positive
            Stage II breast cancer with lymph node involvement
Bone scan: negative to date
Prognosis: tumor board recommends patient is excellent
            candidate for modified radical mastectomy with
            adjunctive chemotherapy: adriamycin and cytoxan

My first dose of chemotherapy is to be on January 2. Happy New Year, Dorothea.

Small glass vials containing the drugs, adriamycin and cytoxan wait in my cold, dark kitchen pantry—all $600 worth of them. I have never once thought about the costs of my treatment: $5,000 for my fourteen days at Boston Hospital for Women; $1,500 for Dr. Dragonas' biopsy and Dr. Shirley's mastectomy. I have health insurance from my newspaper; I wonder what sick people with no insurance do?

The hospital pharmacist told me adriamycin is expensive because it is a relatively new drug. "Oh, yes, it's poisonous," he said. It is so caustic it must be dripped intravenously into the bloodstream, where it has no chance to collect in one place or burn the skin.

"Of course, I will have chemotherapy." That's what I have said over and over to doctors, nurses, friends. "Of course, of course," as if I am afraid of nothing. Like Dr. Deckers, Dr. Shirley believes adjunctive chemotherapy is added insurance. He says, "Twenty years from now you'll be glad you went through it."

The night before my first treatment, I go with Gene to see *The Invasion of the Body Snatchers*. It is a bad choice of movies: people losing control of their own bodies;

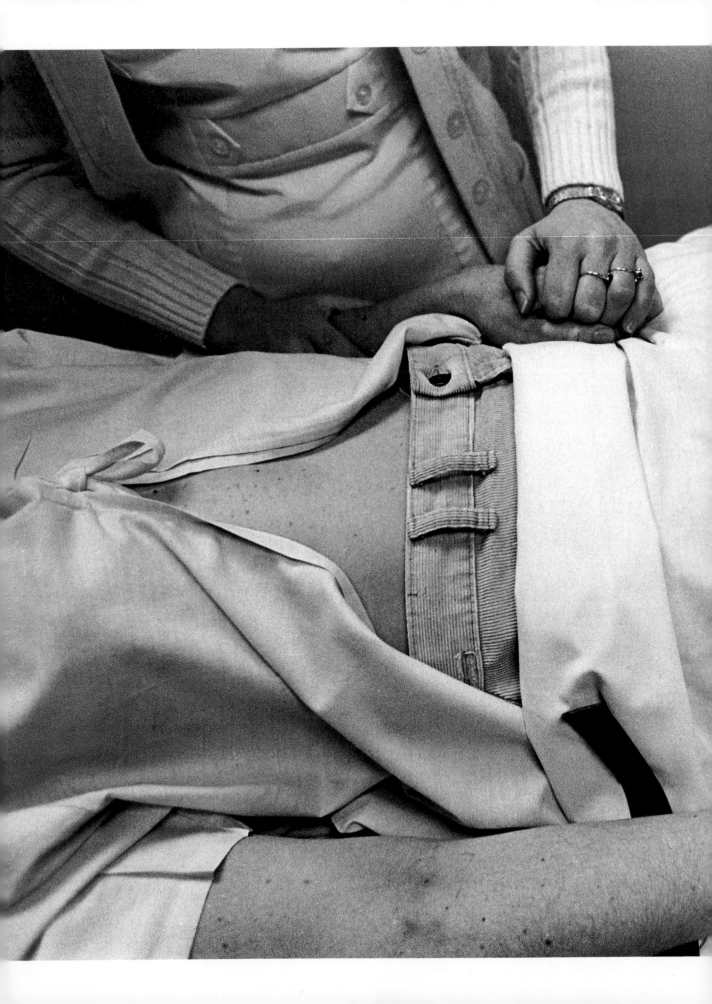

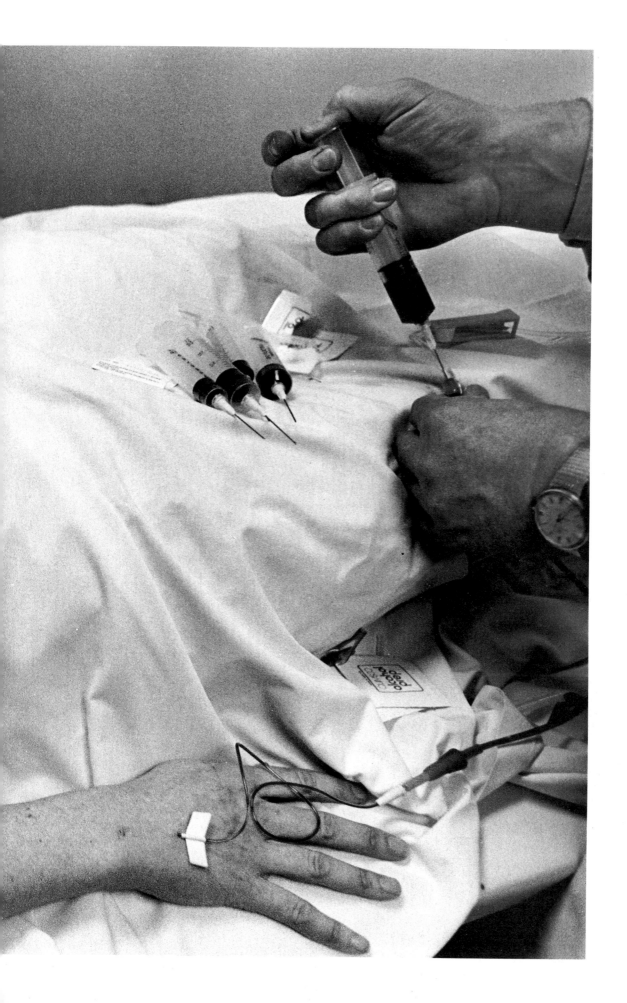

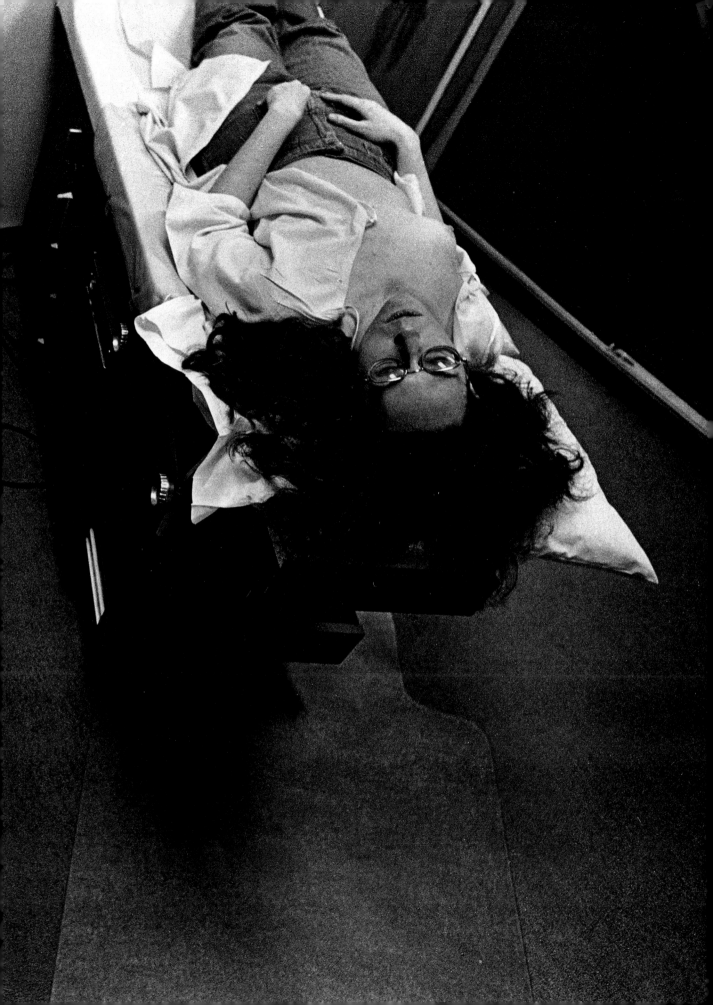

alien plants reproducing cell by cell into duplicate human beings; clinging green tendrils; and everywhere change, change, change.

Dr. Shirley and I go over the chemotherapy procedure for the last time. I will lose all my hair and my menstrual periods may stop. Most people become nauseous, so he prescribes compazine, and he tells me I might get some marijuana and smoke that as well.

I have been doing some reading on my own, too. My cancer textbook tells me how important it is for the patient to receive the maximum dose of chemotherapy drugs each time. Mathematically, it is all beyond me: tumor-killing cells to the tenth power, to the eighth power, to the sixth power. Each time they dose me, they kill the same percentage of cancer cells that are left circling around in my body, until theoretically my own immune system should kick in to polish off the last of the little killers.

So many questions I have forgotten to ask Dr. Shirley. Just how delicate are my cells, and how can I be sure they will return to normal? What are the long-term effect of these poisons? If I ever have a child, could the egg from which it was produced be genetically damaged? Could I produce monsters now?

Dr. Shirley ties the rubber noose tightly across my upper arm, trapping the veins. Boom-bam, boom-bam slams my heart, pouring more blood into my veins, swelling them for the needle's sting.

I hate it. Not even surgery with all its risks and complications seems as deadly as pouring these poisons into my veins. My stomach and bowels tighten with dread. When the doctor touches my hand to encourage me to make a fist, my fingers are ice needles. I cannot stop filling my lungs with air, and still there is not enough oxygen to stave off my fear.

"Oh. Oh, wait," I say, as he begins emptying the syringe. "Oh, what if my heart should fail. Oh, stop. Stop, stop."

"Are you going to be sick?" he asks me.

"No. It's the taste. I can taste the chemical."

They all look at me, Dr. Shirley, Ann the nurse, Margie the aide, and Gene with his camera in his hand, and they wonder what I am talking about. How could I taste the red chemical just beginning to run into my arm? Is my blood already sending a warning to the nerve cells lining the back of my throat, my tongue, all the way to my brain?

I sit on my bathroom floor and lean my head against the cool toilet.

"Poor Dors," Gene says, sitting beside me, wiping my face.

I am angry at being so sick. "Aren't you going to take a picture of this, too?" I snarl at him, as if I were the camera's victim instead of the director.

I throw up every fifteen minutes; I can time it by the commercials that run all night long on the television. Five hours. Eight. Gene falls asleep finally, waking periodically to empty the basin and get me glasses of water. At eleven hours the sky is beginning to lighten, and I think the ordeal will have to end pretty soon. After fifteen hours Gene calls Dr. Shirley's office, and the nurse tells him it should be over soon.

After eighteen hours I stop vomiting. Gene brings me a glass of milk, but I do not dare move, afraid the least motion will set loose the nausea again.

"I don't think I can go through this four more times," I say tearfully to Gene.

"Yes, you will. If I have to carry you there, you will," Gene says grimly.

I am to get my blood drawn, so Dr. Shirley can make sure my white blood count doesn't get too low. "How are you really feeling?" he asks looking quickly at my face. "Not too good, huh? Well, you know we'll be keeping a close watch on your bone marrow activity." I am a little angry at him. "You didn't tell me I would get this sick."

Dr. Shirley leans back in his chair and says to me, "Well, not everybody gets sick. One gal, she was a great gal, a stewardess, we gave her adriamycin and cytoxan, and she never had a sick day in her life. Then, other people are sick before they even get in here. They tell me all they have to do is walk down that corridor.

"You're only going to have five treatments over a dozen weeks, some people are randomized to get ten. In the beginning, they used to give fifteen treatments, but it was too toxic. Cardiomyopathy."

Randomized? Cardiomyopathy? I love him, but Dr. Shirley drives me crazy when he begins talking medicalese. Words that I have to puzzle through, making me feel like a kid trying to talk with grown-ups. I ask him if he means something could go wrong with my heart. Does he mean that I can't run or that I will have heart problems when I get older?

"No," he says, "cardiomyopathy is a rather fast process, and people who have had too many treatments are affected right away—on the table."

I ask him what randomized means and wonder why I have not been told any of this before. Dr. Shirley explains that each cancer patient's case is discussed by a board of oncology specialists, and then all the information available is fed into a computer, which in turn selects "an appropriate regimen."

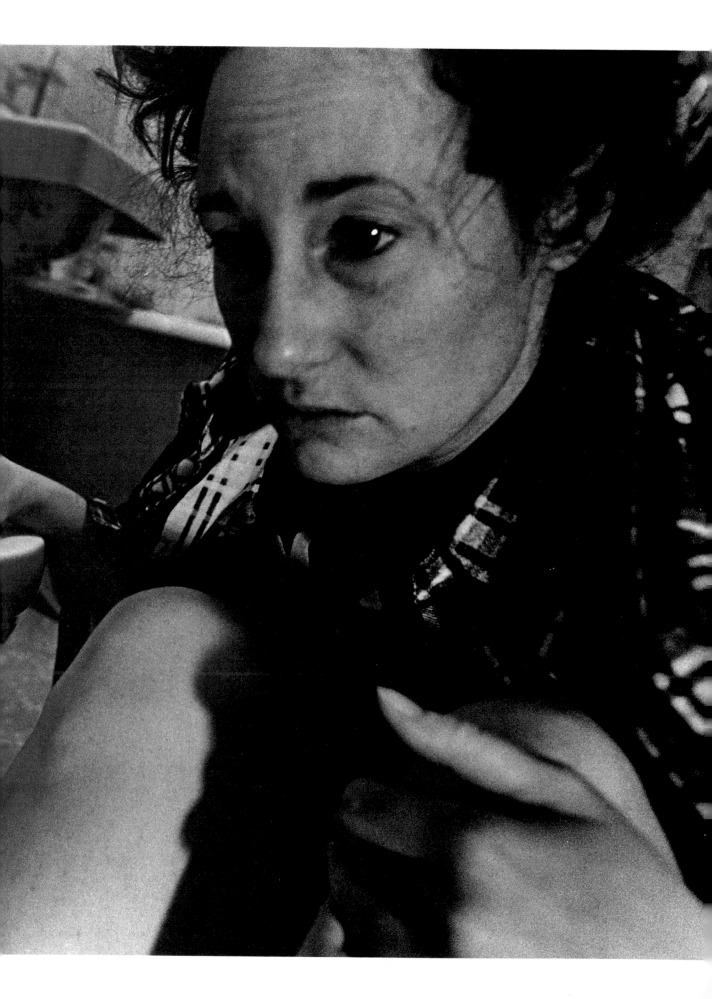

"For instance, some breast cancer patients have been randomized for external beam radiotherapy. But you haven't been. That doesn't mean we're holding back anything. We just don't know whether adjuvant radiation will affect the long-term prognosis. That's what the studies are for. After a certain length of time, we will have sufficient clinical data."

We're guinea pigs, I think to myself, horrified by his coolness. What if they find radiation does prolong life, and I am not going to get any.

"That doesn't seem fair," I say to him, trying to hold back my anger. "That doesn't seem fair at all."

My dresses and my coats have long brown hairs on them now, and my pillow looks like a shedding animal has spent the night on it. My own hairs end up in my mouth. I can't seem to keep my hands away from it. I use my fingers like a rake, stirring and stirring, and the soft curls come away in my hands without a struggle.

"I better get a wig," I say to Gene, "right after this treatment, or I'll freeze to death."

"Smoking marijuana would be a good idea," says Dr. Shirley, grinning, his eyes wide as a child's. He makes me laugh, and I kid him, calling him a dope peddler.

"Really," he says, serious again. "Marijuana might control the nausea caused by the chemotherapy. Are you sure you can get some? If not, there's a hospital where it might be available." I tell Dr. Shirley that my brother has given me an ounce of grass, which looks to me like enough for ten treatments, though, in the past, smoking grass has made me anxious, not calm.

They look for a vein in my right arm. "Damn," says Dr. Shirley. "Looks like I blew that one. We seem to have run out of veins over here. You're not very vain today, my dear."

I wish I could respond with a smile, but I am trying not to cry. Dr. Shirley reminds me to breathe in the Zen way. "Pretend the air is water and you are going to fill your lungs like a pitcher. Concentrate on filling it slowly, beginning from your stomach up to your chest."

I imagine my lungs a lusterware pitcher. He is slapping the veins in my hand, squeezing my cold paw between his, trying to make one of those hidden rivers rise.

Gene rubs my forehead with his fingers. His right hand is wrapped around his camera. He makes little circles on my skin, scattering the sweat above my eyebrows. "It won't be much longer now," he whispers.

The aide clucks deep in her throat at my distress and strokes my free hand, my arm. Dr. Shirley gently rubs my cheek and my head. He does not seem to notice I am getting bald. "Only three more to go," he says.

The television flickers all night long in the bedroom, turning the walls purple. I want to do nothing but rest in between bouts of vomiting, but every few minutes the voice of an announcer pricks at my consciousness. I try to understand what he's talking about: "Three Mile Island . . . damaged fuel rods . . . Three Mile Island." I throw up and throw up, making little sense of it all.

Three days later, I am able to get up, shaky and depressed, like someone who is recovering from the flu. There is my dressing to be changed, and I try unsuccessfully to wrap the bandage myself. More of my hair has fallen out, and it is caught in choked little balls that itch my scalp like Brillo pads. I get on the bathroom scale. "Six pounds," I say to Gene. "I've lost six pounds. At least there's one good thing about all this."

My hairdresser Ron says he will try to cut the hairballs away so I will be more comfortable. The salon where he works on Newbury Street is full of mirrors and pictures of beautiful women. I catch sight of myself as Ron begins tugging a little at the clumps of hair.

"I'm afraid I won't be able to make it look like much," he says, shaking his head over the destruction. "Are you going to lose all of it? That's terrible."

I am glad no one tries to cheer me up or tell me how beautiful I will look once my hair grows back. None of the saleswomen demonstrating make-up approach me, and no one except a few late-arriving customers look at me at all. I think Ron has warned everyone ahead of time, and I am grateful.

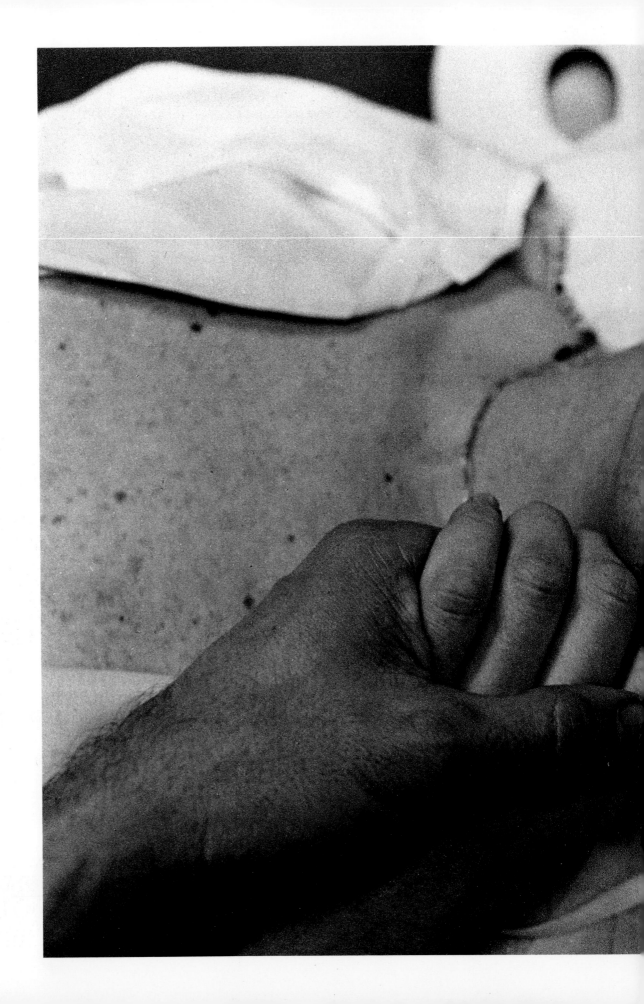

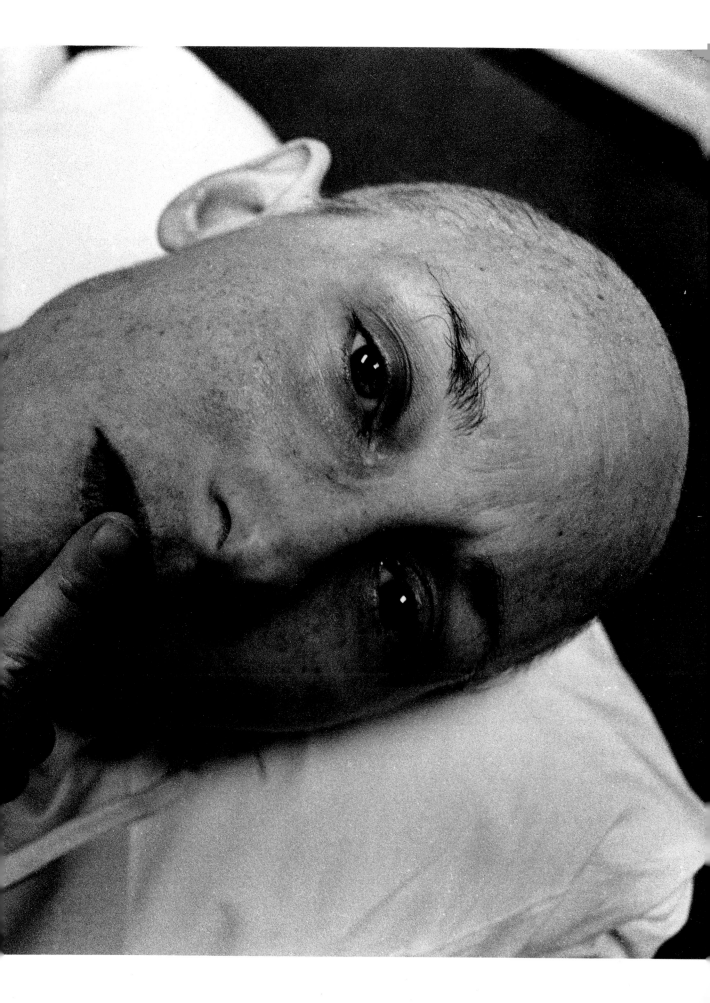

The back of my neck, where my hair used to be, is cold. Gene and I ask directions to stores that sell wigs. At the Wig Warm, the salesgirl offers me a private booth with a curtain, but I just want to hurry up and find something at least a little like my own frizzy hair.

"What's that?" I ask, pointing to a cloud of brown synthetic hair that resembles an airdale's fur.

"Oh, that's our punk wig. It comes in blue, too."

When I try the brown one on everyone laughs. It looks terrific, as if I just had my own hair permed into an early forties style.

After making the purchase we walk along Temple Street. It is beginning to rain, but I am comfortable and warm, especially my head. Two businessmen come toward us and one checks me out, turning around and looking after us. "Look at that," I say to Gene nudging him, "I must look pretty cute, after all."

I look at myself in the bathroom mirror when I am home alone. Bald; lashless; eyebrowless; scaly patches of red, dry skin all over my face; thick, blackened scar tissue where my breast once was. I am dried up, older than ancient, sexless. My body is unfamiliar territory to me, and if I have any great sorrow it is that my body is unreliable now.

At the photography school in New York where Gene teaches part-time, a few people shyly ask how I am, and others look sideways at me. A teacher, who had written me several times when I was in the hospital, looks at me and walks away. Maybe she doesn't recognize me in the wig, and I have lost some weight.

But this woman is not unlike the photographer who telephoned a few weeks ago, warning Gene of the dangers of living with a cancer patient. "Are you going to keep living together?" she asked. "I mean ... well, it's transferred from saliva."

"What is?"

"Cancer. That's how people get leukemia—they get it from saliva."

"Where the hell did you get that idea?" Gene screamed at her. "You're talking about cat leukemia, cat's saliva. A disease of cats, not people. Cats."

One of Gene's students at the school asks to see the pictures Gene has made of my hospital stay. "Do you have a different attitude now?" the student asks me, the photographs spread on the table between us. "Aren't you going to change your lifestyle?"

"I couldn't have a much healthier lifestyle," I tell him. "I ran, I'm a vegetarian, and I stopped smoking four years ago. What else am I to do?"

"Yes, but it's your attitude that's important," he says earnestly. "There are all kinds of studies that show cancer patients repress feelings and emotions."

I know what he is talking about. He's saying people cause their own cancers by having the wrong emotions or reactions, sort of the old philosophy of blaming the victim.

I would like to give his pseudo-radical ponytail a good yank. Ever since I've been in the hospital, well-meaning friends and people I barely know have flooded me with bibles, tracts on holistic therapy, macrobiotic diets, each person wanting to be the one with the answer, the cure. They made me hopeful at first, then tired, tired.

My last chemotherapy treatment is approaching, and I wish I were brave enough to say stop, enough. I wonder if they are really telling me the truth when they say I have a good prognosis. If I ask, Dr. Shirley will patiently review the five-year, ten-year, twenty-year statistics, but that isn't what I want to hear. Does Gene know the truth? I want Dr. Shirley to come hold me with his big warm hands and tell me everything is like before. No more cancer, no more changes.

The third chemo was delivered through a fragile vein in my right hand after unsuccessful attempts in my forearm and arm on Valentine's Day—not my idea of a valentine for a nice lady. On the way back to the apartment, Gene stopped at a flower shop to buy me a green and purple orchid. I turned the delicate beauty around and around, holding it by its little glass vial, afraid that putting it against my skin would discolor the petals.

My periods have stopped. I shouldn't be surprised since Dr. Shirley warned me that the chemicals usually disturb the monthly process. But I am never late. I keep returning to the bathroom, pressing a piece of white toilet paper against my vagina; it remains unstained.

What does this shutting down mean? For twenty-two years I have been influenced by the rhythms of my physical self: the fluids of sex running and swelling hidden tissues; the dull ache in my lower abdomen that changes sides from one month to another as the infinitesimal egg bursts free and drops into the tube; the pale spot of pink on my underpants, like a careless lipstick stain.

60

I sit on the toilet, crying for the children I would now never dream of starting. I read somewhere that woman is born with a precise number of unfertilized eggs in her ovaries, carrying them through her years of doll-playing, roller-skating, dating. Millions of waiting seeds that are growing old along with me and are taking in the poisons that circle through my body every three weeks. A child from one of those eggs?

An article in this month's *Scientific American* theorizes about the uncertain effects of chemotherapeutic drugs, drugs so toxic they may be capable of generating new tumors in the patient's body. The book we have on cancer medicine puts it another way: "...The evidence, at present, suggests that ... [cessation of menses], per se, is not associated with subsequent abnormalities of the children of such patients if conception occurs. However, in the young male patient, with a testicular tumor, it is worth considering sperm storage prior to chemotherapy."

This is it: the fifth and last treatment. I am surprised that I feel so little relief, perhaps because I know I still have one last sickness to get through.

"Hey," Gene says, holding up his camera, "we should get a picture of this. This is a celebration."

I sit on the edge of Dr. Shirley's examining table, already nauseated, and smile back at Gene. I don't know what to do or how to look. Finally, I hold up the Amazon T-shirt Gene has given me, remembering what my friend Hollysue said to me in the hospital. "Now, you're like one of those legendary women warriors—an Amazon. They cut off one breast so they can shoot better with a bow and arrow."

Spring again. I will be thirty-five next week. So much has passed between the operation and today; I don't even feel like the same person.

I am almost ashamed to say it, but I can never remember being so happy. Friends and family still call it euphoria or bravery, but it is none of those things. The woman who was terrified of death and what she thought its ugliest manifestation—cancer— of changes, of being without choice or will has survived the confrontation. Cancer is a disease of life, not death. My world is upside down, and I do not know what will survive from this strange new knowledge.

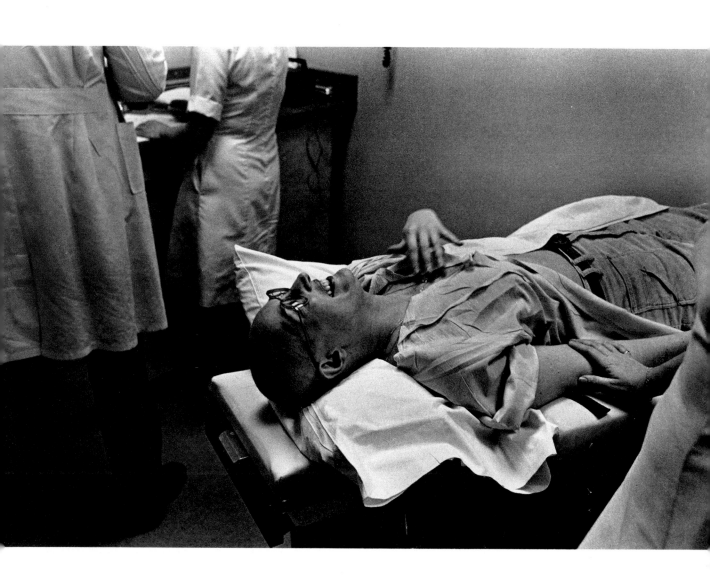

In May I take off my wig once and for all and throw it in the trash: an act of faith. My own hair is still just a soft bristle, and when I return to my job on the *Patriot Ledger* people smile at me and sometimes even run their palms over the top of my head.

My first assignment is to cover the Holbrook High School graduation ceremonies. Bright beautiful day, graduates in flapping robes with cameras, hundreds of happy faces. But, over to one side, there is a group of townies who have caught sight of me. They whisper, laugh, then point. Other people turn to see the source of the joke.

"Hare, Hare Krishna. Hare, Hare Rama," they begin to sing the words at me, as if, by virtue of my haircut, I were a member of the Hare Krishna sect. They are seeing something out of the ordinary and they are eager for a little blood.

I feel the wind in my hair—"Hare, Hare Krishna"—and I am embarrassed and finally angry, angry the way I was last week at Carson Beach when an elderly couple turned and stared at me, and a woman who could have been my grandmother muttered, "bull dyke," as I walked past her.

The boys watch as I approach, their smiles shrinking, hands jammed into pockets. They shift from one foot to another.

"Do you know why I look like this?" I say to their smug sixteen-year-old faces. "I have cancer, and I had to have treatments that made my hair fall out. How do you think that makes me feel? I hope no one in your family ever gets cancer and is treated the way you are treating me today."

The boys put their heads down, red in the face, and move back silently.

In July, Gene and I take a vacation at a tiny lakeside cottage in Maine. Adams Lake is full of fat goldfish and water-walkers. I go for my first mile run in eight months, my sneakers slapping against the bare Maine dirt. When I stop to catch my breath Gene makes a picture of my blood-filled cheeks.

Sunshine, long walks, swimming: this is the kind of Maine vacation I used to share twenty-five years ago with my family. I remember us as we were then and realize my mother must have been nearly the same age I am now. I am standing where my parents once stood, in the middle of life.

Gene and I sleep on the screen porch, which as a child I was never allowed to do. All night, moths, big as flowers, hang on the screens.

THREE

After being examined at Dr. Shirley's, I drive along Soldier's Field Road toward Boston, the green roadsigns easier to see without the rain falling. Alone, singing to myself, down past the Cadillac-Olds sign that hangs upside down in the Charles. Trees and the lights from hundreds of buildings swim in the old river, and directly over the city, the sky is clearing in a circle around a full moon.

It is almost too perfect, a child's dream of a summer night. When I was ten or twelve I was overwhelmed by evenings when honeysuckle grew along with the moonlight. Hair streaming out behind me, I would ride down Bushnell and Carruth and Van Winkle Streets with my feet up on the front fender of my bike, free of the wildly spinning pedals. Swooping from one gutter to another, heading for the lower half of Adams Street where it curved around the cemetery, with its monuments like pointing fingers, towards Dorchester Park. The dark streets deep into August, the whirr of rubber tires, the tic-tic-tic-tic-tic of spinning spokes. Anything could happen, would happen. Tonight, driving home alone along the river, I'm touched by that old excitement.

"Okay, feet together and bend, ten times. Feet apart, touch the elbow of one arm to the opposite knee, twenty times . . . Now lift your leg as high as you can, fifteen times each side."

My legs are trembling. My whole body shakes, and I feel the trickle of sweat along my neck and under my arms. This class is my friend Joyce's discovery. She thinks it will help her lose weight and make me stronger. A back sprain had lasted two

68

weeks. Unable to stand longer than ten minutes, I felt fat and lazy—and afraid. It was the inevitable reaction to unexplained pain. The little jolt of fear under the breastbone, a rush of hot blood. Oh, no. Not a tumor.

The instructor brays out one order after another: "Hands on hips, deep knee bends, ten times ." My heart pounds, stutters. Sweating and panting, the other women fix their mouths into determined lines.

From time to time Joyce yells over at me, "How ya doing?" I am embarrassed to tell her how scared I am of collapsing in the middle of a high kick—the gasps of surprise, the curious onlookers. After all this, to die of a heart attack! Then, I am jumping. Jumping jacks, legs splayed, hands clapping over my head in time with the rhythm of a rock song. My heart resumes its race, and I feel a rush of power in my legs, my back, the tips of my fingers. The song and its energy are inside me. "Da-dum, da-dum, da-dum," I sing to myself. "Oh, I am strong. I am strong. I am STRONG."

Over a drink Joyce tells me that I look good. "Actually, you look beautiful," she says. I know she is not talking about my new hair or the loss of weight.

I would like to tell her that I'm not just beautiful, but stunning, that having one breast doesn't lessen the image I have of myself as a woman. But the sexual me isn't convinced of this yet.

"Do you think the scar's ugly?" I ask Gene as we lay side by side on our bed. Girls sunbathing on Carson Beach and a shapely woman that Gene looked after on the street crowd into my sleep, swaying their bodies.

"Do you think I'm ugly?"

Gene doesn't answer my questions, but groans, "Be quiet," and pulls me tight, up against him.

My mother telephones in the morning to say she is continuing to pray for my total recovery. Everyone, I suppose, expects me to pick up just where I left off before getting sick—emotions under control, outlook bright. As if now that I have visited the prosthesis lady and received my rubber tit, everything can go on as it was.

But I don't want everything the way it was. I am happier and more desperate than ever before. Balancing on an edge so sharp I could cut myself against it. Though doctors, months ago, plucked out my tumor and burned away any renegade cells, I cannot leave the disease behind me.

Cancer haunts me. News articles dealing with cancer's causes and cancer's cures overflow my files. I pore over the morning obituaries to see how many people have "died of cancer," "died following a long illness," "died after a lengthy battle." Floating at the edge of my brain are glimpses of a tumid world, taking hold within the larger universe that is me, Dorothea.

The fears come when I'm writing a news story or falling asleep in the bathtub. I ran a mile tonight along Carson Beach, with the wind in my face. Still they came on—memory flashes of knives and needles, of a black bag filled with unconsciousness.

Vietnam veterans are on television tonight talking of having frequent bouts of depression and terrifying dreams, how their lives are being bent and broken by experiences that happened to them years ago. "Post-Vietnam syndrome," doctors call it, death in life. "You know," Gene says, getting up from the couch, "it isn't so different for you." God knows, of course, this cancer of mine is not over. I'm scared and I'm confused. Maybe a little crazed. My mother and some of my friends have even suggested that for my own good I give up thinking and writing so much about cancer. But I can't stop, don't dare stop. If I am ever to gain control over my life and contribute something to other people, I must learn more and more about the "big C." Anyway, I would be better off knowing, rather than not knowing, what the future could hold for me.

The bronze plaques and framed certificates on the white walls are honors from the Harvard Medical School. The photographs are of politicians. Before ushering us into an inner office, a receptionist makes it clear that we are intruding on a busy schedule and an important life.

"What do you expect to do with all your writing?" asks the eminent oncologist. "Of course, it's probably a good way to exorcise some of your feelings."

"No, I'm a journalist," I answer, trying to sound confident but feeling as if I were reciting for a grade school teacher. "Gene and I want to research how it is for others who live with cancer."

I pray that the doctor will look over the excerpts from my cancer diary and Gene's photographs and say to us, "Who could refuse you?" Instead, he acts as if a gun is being pointed at him. Without moving out from behind the desk, he turns down our request to work with his cancer patients.

For months now we have been battering against the doors of officialdom, writing letters, meeting with hospital administrators, board members, lawyers, public relations people, and more than two dozen doctors. What could be more natural, I had thought, than a cancer patient wanting to write about other cancer patients.

Dr. Lawrence, oncologist and board member at Boston Hospital for Women, is horrified at the idea of our making "intimate" photographs of his patients. In a letter he circulates to fellow physicians he claims that Gene had asked to photograph a woman having a vaginal implant as treatment for her cancer. He calls Gene a pornographer. When we ask my old gynecologist for help he sees "no need to rock the boat." Other doctors beg previous commitments or offer to act as their patients' mouthpieces rather than let us meet with them in person. We are told that even if patients agree to work with us our writing and photography will still compromise their "right to privacy." "Patients' right to privacy" is cited again and again as the reason for keeping us out until I cry in frustration. Jesus, it's not a secret illness, one out of three Americans will get cancer. I cannot understand the mistrust, this opposition to us.

"Patients' right to privacy." When I hear these words, I think of the heavy drapes that screen hospital beds. The drapes that shield patients from bright lights and the wantonly curious can also be pulled tight to muffle protest and shut patients away from the world.

In desperation, we contact Dr. Peter Deckers at University Hospital. Dr. Deckers, who had advised me last November on my own cancer, listens to us, really listens. After taking a deep breath, he exclaims, "Why not?" His thunderous voice booms even louder, "Why the hell not? Maybe we will all learn something."

I want to hug him, kiss him, but he gets a phone call from one patient, then another. "Oh, thank you," I blurt out, as we back out the door. Gene and I dance down the hall to see the head social worker, whom we are told will coordinate our work with patients. But Joan Williams is long-faced and vague. She says that while she does appreciate Decker's enthusiasm for educational projects, many patients will not feel up to being interviewed and photographed. We must wait, she says. Wait for the right time, wait for the right patient.

Close to midnight I put on lipstick and go out by myself to the Victoria for a drink. I sit at a table with my book.

Gene and I are fighting again.

It seems as if the fight has been going on for the entire sixteen years we have know each other, with slight variations, whenever we are suffering from the greatest disappointments.

"Why aren't you writing more?" Gene asks. "Why don't you write down what's been going on?"

"I don't know."

"What keeps you from writing?"

"I don't know. The enormity of it."

Can't he understand that my self-confidence is unraveling? What does cancer mean? Mean to whom? And who cares anyway? How can I be taking this on? I have no medical education. What if I get onto the cancer ward and find myself with nothing to say?

"Dammit, you know this isn't easy for me, either," Gene says. "Waiting for the goddamn doctors. Waiting for the right patient. And the photographs are hard on me to make."

I suppose they are. At Boston Hospital for Women, Gene held the camera in front of his face while my stitches were examined, and I tried to exercise the painful block of flesh that was my left arm. When he took the camera down, I could see tears of tiredness and fear. Still, tonight I am not feeling any sympathy for him.

We go to sleep almost hating each other.

He awakens me by rubbing his beard on my cheek. He pushes my hair back from my forehead and brings two Anacins for my headache. Still, I can't return his "good morning." I stare, goading him with my reticence, seeing the veins stand out in his temple as if the skin can barely contain the blood rushing beneath. There is a fragility about him, hands that make me think of a bird cage or skeleton, so little flesh over a quivering nervous system.

God, what I wouldn't give to have the work with cancer patients underway. Over. Finished. Done. The argument last night was just the latest round. Friday night I was left wide awake, crying, after our frustrations ignited more personal unhappiness. I lay awake until dawn beside a man I do not always know, who changes from intense sweetness to strident need, to cold dismissal, to frustrated rage.

I'm appalled by my own selfishness in the face of his generosity this morning. But I can't help it. When we argue, old fears surface and take control. Last year we were close to splitting up. Unable to find enough work, feeling inept, uncreative, anxious, he began to blame me. Then there were one, two, three—how many women did he juggle in his head? It's ending, ending I thought. He doesn't want to live the life we have had for all these years.

Gene comes back into the bedroom carrying a steaming cup of coffee for me. His casual, confident air has vanished, and he looks like a little boy in pain.

"I'm sorry," he says, "about last night. I don't know why I do it, blow up all around you when what is upsetting me has nothing to do with you."

I listen to him, recalling that the moon outside our window last night was angry and red, thin—thin as my mouth is feeling—a repressed, little sliver of a moon. The morning light coming into our bedroom, though, is silvery and calm. I ask Gene if he would like to share my cup of coffee.

His neck is wet with sweat after running two miles, his legs shining out of purple shorts, my shorts. Gene stretches out on the living room floor. When he catches his breath, he does sit-ups and lifts one hundred pounds of iron weights over his head. At each push, his arms tremble. Tiny boned, once a fat kid, he has always wanted to be strong.

I stare at him. It is an arresting face, a combination of severity and sexuality: full lips, beard cut close to his face, eyes wrinkled at the corners from years of squinting. The wrinkles are deepening and his hair has receded making his forehead a prominent feature the bony surfaces of his skull visible.

He's thirty-five years old now, but looking at him I remember the way we were long ago. It was fourteen years ago, on a day off from college, that Gene and I went on our first shopping trip together, bringing back stone wheat crackers, brie, and pistachio nuts, eating them in my bedroom. I pretended we were artists living together, until I heard the sound of my mother's key in the front door.

Ten years ago, if asked, I probably would have said that the most important thing about me was my relationship with the man I loved. For I was feeling then that my own vision of the world, my politics, my writing, even the words I spoke had little value. After winning a writing award in college, I couldn't write, and didn't finish another poem for almost two years.

When Gene joined VISTA after college, I went on to graduate school and wrote page after page of poetry, but I couldn't get free of the menacing, immobilizing fear that I was only posing as a writer. Looking back I see that my poems from 1969 had little relevance to the times at hand. I did carry a candle in a peace ceremony with a few hundred other students, and I remember a party where I got drunk and listened to a woman crying over the students shot at Kent State, but mostly I watched and was silent as the whirlwind passed by.

A month after leaving grad school, aching for experience, I loaded up my old Pontiac and drove south to West Memphis, Arkansas. West Memphis, a farming town at the edge of the Mississippi River, was home base for Respect, Inc., the social-action organization that Gene helped build after leaving VISTA.

In the raw nerve months that followed, the sheltered schoolgirl poet met the desperately poor people of the delta plantations who were hungry, living in bone ugly shacks, wearing rags. I worked as a bookkeeper at a chemical company to support Gene and myself, carried sick children to the county health clinic, wrote news stories about police brutality and the Ku Klux Klan for the Respect newspaper.

One Christmas eve I brought toys to a family I found huddled together in bed for warmth; they were saving their few bits of firewood for Christmas day.

Life, finally, was upon me. But quickly it became more brutal than I could have imagined. Friends were beaten by Klan sympathizers, pet dogs were shot, the gas was turned on in our house, the wheel lugs of my car were loosened. One Sunday morning I found Gene bloody and dazed after a man cut him up with razor blades, and I felt such hatred for his assailant I could have killed him. I began to have nightmares about guns exploding from parked cars, about a man aiming a shotgun at our front window. Exhausted and confused, I was coming apart. I returned to Boston, skirting a nervous breakdown. Harassed by local police, his organization failing, Gene reluctantly followed six months later.

I always picture Dorchester as I see it from the subway train: wooden three-deckers, old streets angling away from the tracks, lines of yellow school buses, black faces pressed to the windows, bits of life on the streets after the kids have been sent off to school, the toys, the lines of washing, lots of dogs. On the way downtown to talk again to Dr. Deckers, we go by failed and failing factories and my mother's school of fifty years ago, St. Peter's, high on a hill.

Living here most of my life, I thought I knew Dorchester well, indoors and out. But in recent months I've been reseeing, reevaluating my old home—how all the shabby buildings; the crowds of people; the clumps of trees; the brown, gray, blue, and black skies are in transition. I sit close to Gene on the subway. Fragments of my childhood come to me in a startling rush as Dorchester slides by . . .

Quarter of seven. I am going to read a poem to my seventh grade classmates today. Time to get up. I like to be the first one out of bed and into the bathroom. I scrub my face with soap and splash water in the wash basin until bubbles like ginger ale break the surface.

My mother is hurrying along the hall in a pink nightgown. "Good morning," I call to her. She stares at me as if she has forgotten my name. She has no slippers on. She stumbles on the stairs and catches the railing.

"What's the matter? Mum? Mummy?"

My father lies in the bed, a blue blanket stretched smoothly across his chest. There's little color in his face. I move quietly, waiting for his eyes to open, his teeth to shine.

"Daddy is sick," I tell my sister, who stands on the third stair down, her arms clasped against her chest.

"Daddy is dead," she snaps back at me.

My Aunt Jule arrives with Uncle George. Aunt Flo hugs me, wiping tears from her face. Auntie Ellen is putting a ham and frozen turkey into the refrigerator. Whiskey bottles and cups of coffee cover the kitchen table. There are the sounds of shuffling feet, a thud, creaking steps. The men who are carrying my father down from the third floor are breathing hard. My Aunt Jule says, "Why don't you go outside into the sun?"

But there is nothing to do. There is no point in being outside when there is nothing to do. It's too hot in the sun, too cold in the shade.

Roses, winter-chill carnations, the spiky, pale points of gladiolas, and in the midst of them all, my mother in a new dress. I remember her saying that the smell of carnations sickens her; I watch to see if she will throw up. My grandmother catches hold of my arm and pushes me towards the open coffin, her nails leaving half moons on my skin. "Pray for your father," she says.

I turn in the humid night, winding the bedclothes around myself. Awakened in the darkness, my mother rousing me in the winter morning, "Dress quickly, hurry, let's hurry."

"Where are we going, mummy?"

"Don't you remember? You're going to the hospital so the doctor can make your tonsils better."

I lie still, swallow hard, trying to clear my head of sleep and dreams. Gene has to pull me to my feet. "The alarm's gone off. It's 4:30."

Dawn is just a golden streak in the sky when we park our car outside University Hospital. The guard at the front desk checks the identity cards pinned to our coats. The photos show us smiling, aware of our new, officially recognized status. We have been approved to work with patients after all these long, long months. "Made it," we say to each other as we head for the elevators to C-5. C building, fifth floor. C for Cancer.

A rustle of sheets, a moan running down into a snore, one wet cough that goes on and on. At 5:30 in the morning the cancer ward is a no-man's land. The corridor is dim, lined with dark rectangles that are the doors to patients' rooms. Out of the rooms drift the odors of antiseptic, urine, alcohol, the perspiration and breath of a dozen sick people.

We tiptoe along the hall. Gene carries his camera over his shoulder, and I clutch a new notebook as if it were a permission slip. Dr. Deckers, bless him, has arranged for us to go on rounds. Waiting is his amiable chief resident, Dr. Bill Kelley, and a handful of interns and students who look us over warily. At 5:45 we begin.

There are two purposes for making rounds I've been told. One is to check on the condition of patients, the other is for medical students to see and discuss real-life cases. The group files into Mr. Nichols's room. Fearful of saying or doing something inappropriate, Gene and I hang back in the doorway. I look at Mr. Nichols, a middle-aged man who has a virulent form of blood cancer. I think of Gene's photo of me after surgery with a terrified face and watery eyes, and I feel helpless. Bill Kelley checks the chart and asks Mr. Nichols if he is in any pain. Then he waves Gene and me forward near the side of the bed.

Mr. Nichols holds out his hand for me to clasp. The exhausted, gray face breaks into a smile. "A story about us would be a wonderful thing," he says. "But we must hurry if I'm to be involved. I'm leaving in a few days to get married."

At this news the medical students and interns crowd closer, whooping out loud and shaking hands with Mr. Nichols and with each other. Everyone is laughing, telling marriage jokes. The good spirit is contagious. Two interns introduce themselves, and promise to assist us in understanding other patients' cancer. A medical student puts his arm around my shoulder and welcomes me aboard.

"You mean Marguerite? That tiny Spanish woman?"

"That's right. She's in the hospital . . . cancer."

Waiting for the elevator, trying to catch my breath, I eavesdrop on some women, big women, black, with lots of teased hair, white shoes—hospital workers on the way home from their shift.

"They took her voice box."

"Oh, no."

"Lordy. Lordy."

The fact is, I am tired and a bit unnerved. The head social worker just cautioned us again not to impose on patients, though nearly all the patients we've met, tagging along behind the doctors, are, like Mr. Nichols, hungry for contact and eager to tell their stories.

"Took her voice box away."

"Isn't that terrible. Why, if her mother knew, she would just die."

"When she was a kid, that girl wanted for nothing. She didn't turn out the way her mother wanted her to. She wanted her to have everything."

"Things just don't turn out that way."

"What would you do if that were you, Marie?"

Marie is thoughtful. She shakes her head, moans, and finally chuckles out loud, "Rather take me than that old voice box."

Clistee Boles thinks of herself as Gene's confidant. She looks forward to his visits and giggles when the nurses tell her she will become as big a star as her favorite actress on *General Hospital*. While Mrs. Boles watches soap operas, every afternoon from 1 to 4, Gene photographs her. Small-boned and overweight, Mrs. Boles is sunken into the pillow, her round face constantly nodding, smiling—burning with freckles. Strands of reddish hair, like a kewpie doll's, stand up around her head.

Slowly, slowly, Mrs. Boles and I struggle to communicate. Talk: inconsequential talk; talk: monumental—stories of Mrs. Boles's orphaned life, her thirty years on a factory assembly line, her beliefs in otherworldly things—portents, prayers, Good, Evil, heavenly rewards. Words and phrases finally whole paragraphs begin to add up to fifty-nine years of life. She maps out her days for me, as if I have the right to know every detail of the drama out of which she has stepped.

"My daughter, who is seventeen, almost eighteen, is waiting for me to come home, for me to cook a big dinner . . . I took care of myself when I was a kid and grew up like a weed in New Hampshire. I was the second child. My mother died of a ruptured appendix two days after giving birth, so I lived with my aunt and my father who was a cobbler. My father, he had diabetes and lost both legs when he stepped on a tack and it didn't heal . . . I was a good kid. Cute? I don't think so, but everybody liked me. I married at nineteen but to a drunkard. That side of my family, I put out of my mind. It's been a hard life, but I suppose it was worth it. You see,

I'm not a crybaby. I never went to a doctor until after my four kids were born, and two of them were born at home. I never went to the doctor for anything serious, until now."

Mrs. Boles's eldest daughter comes in from the hallway. We are told we must have permission from her in order to continue our interviews. The daughter walks about the hospital room wondering out loud why her mother should want to discuss "the situation" with anyone outside of family. She is like Mrs. Boles, stubborn and plain, a country woman. While Mrs. Boles continually dismisses any mention of the word cancer, the daughter is caught up by the ferociousness of the disease. She fidgets with the IV tube and stares at the bruises on her mother's arm where needles have been slipped beneath the skin.

"It's overwhelming," she says. "Overwhelming." Finally, looking as though she is passing by in a fog, she signs the release.

Mrs. Boles doesn't fear my tape recorder and seems to welcome questions, but she remains reluctant to talk about the nature of "the thing" that has brought her to this hospital. She says she doesn't know the name for her illness or its prognosis. She will leave that kind of information to her doctors.

"What I don't know won't hurt me, I guess. Cancer? No one ever says that. Well, no one ever says the word cancer to me. Maybe they talk behind my back, but I don't . . . I can't . . . I don't believe that's the word. Something gets in there and grows like some people have warts. Why couldn't something get inside you and grow? Lots of people have ulcers and things. I think they frighten people by saying that it is cancer."

Her doctor, Joe Feller, tells us that a tumor the size of a melon was removed from Mrs. Boles's stomach five months ago, but it is growing again. I can see the round lump, the new growth makes beneath her bedclothes. Mrs. Boles watches Dr. Feller as he bends over her and places his hands on her arm, then on her belly. Her eyes are wide with awe, and for the first time since I've met her, she is speechless.

The interns and students who accompany Dr. Feller on rounds watch from the

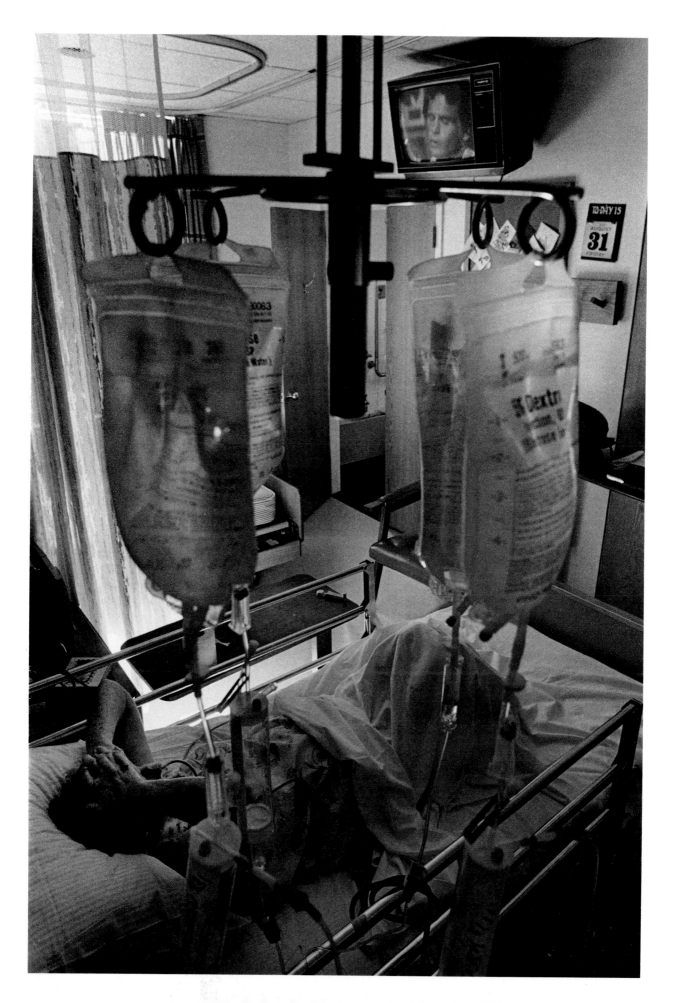

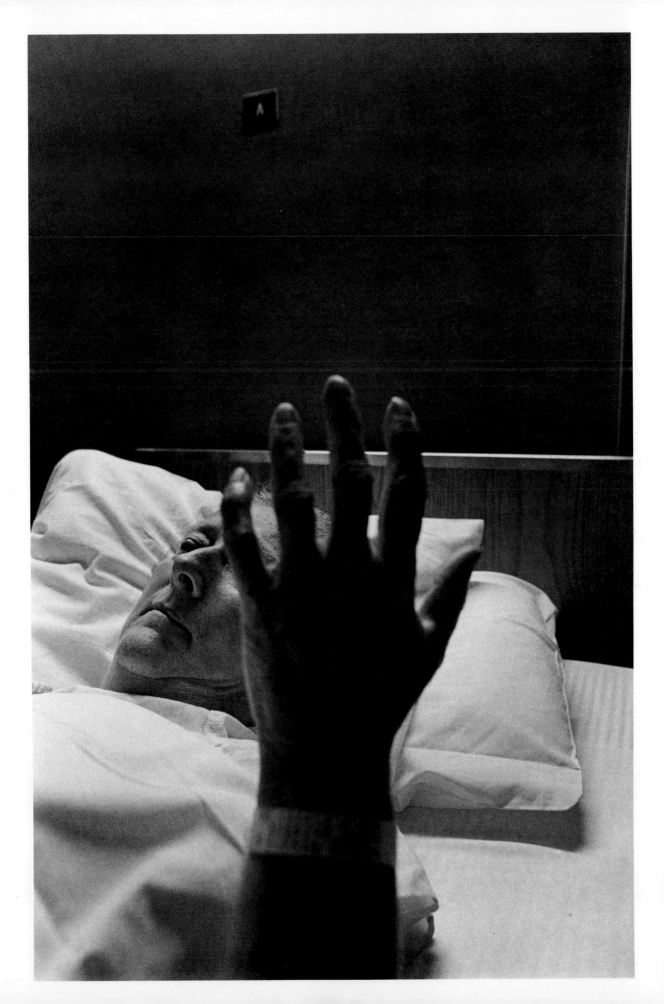

sidelines half-heartedly. They are not concerned with the persona of this frightened, middle-aged woman whose life is circumscribed by the day-to-day activities of her doctor, her daughters, and her favorite TV stars. They are interested only in tomorrow morning's surgery to save her life.

It is very hot. My surgical dress has short sleeves but they bind. The dress itself is too short; the material strains at my waist. We put on throwaway shoe covers and ugly flowered paper caps, so silly on top of the men's heads that patients stare and make nervous jokes about them.

And finally the mask. Now we know it is for real. Today we are going beyond the silver door—so like the door to a meat locker—into the operating room. But no, the patient isn't Mrs. Boles but a woman named Mrs. Burke. After granting Gene and me permission to attend Clistee Boles's surgery, Dr. Feller had second thoughts. His once friendly face closed to our questions and excitement. This operation on Mrs. Boles, a nurse tells us, will be Dr. Feller's first as a member of the permanent oncology department, so only staff will be in attendance.

The mask is confining and throws nervous-smelling breath back in my face. I wonder if our breath and the patient's breath have the same taint of fear? Mrs. Burke has already been taken inside Operating Room One. If I look through the little square of glass on the door, I can see the anesthesiologist already at work. Gene follows the O.R. nurse into the room, a camera over each shoulder and one around his neck. Dr. Kelley is finished scrubbing up at the sink. It cannot be put off any longer. There is nothing left to do but follow them in. I check my pocket for the ampoule of ammonia I have brought along to counter my tendency to faint.

The heart monitor is beeping. Mrs. Burke's face is covered with a black mask that pours oxygen and anesthetic into her lungs. Her chest rises up and down, and her breathing is so deep, almost a snore.

There are five O.R.s in a row, like mechanics' bays but without the grease. Even though it is small, our operating room is hard to take in all at once. Clean green

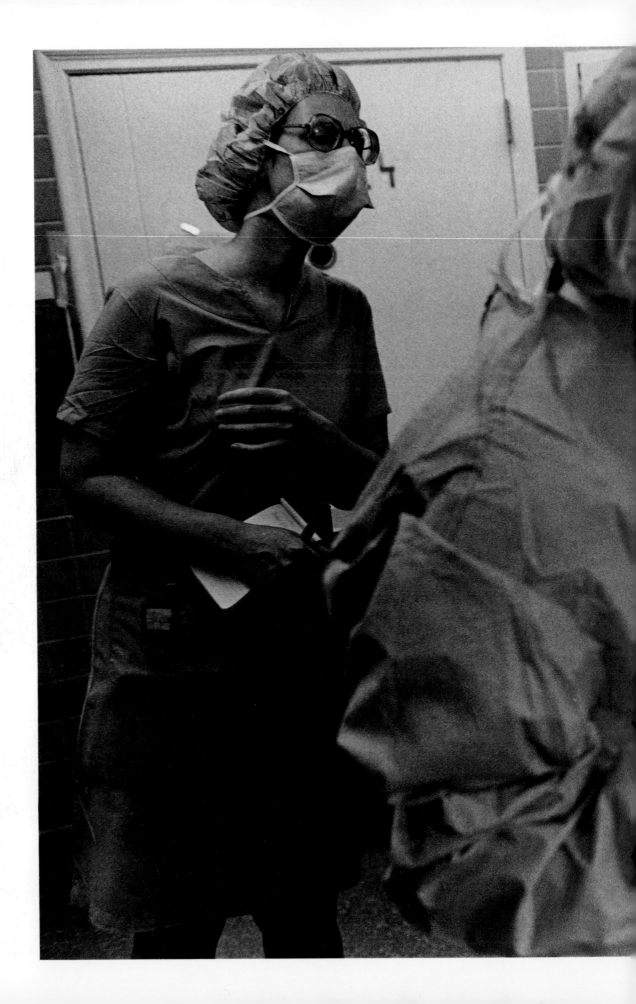

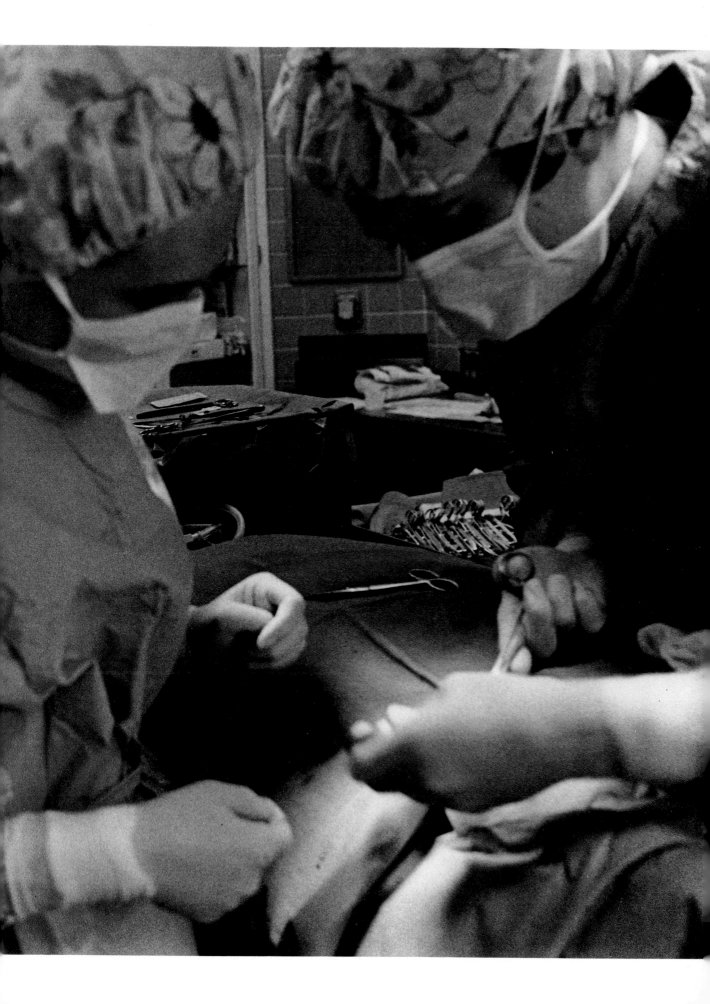

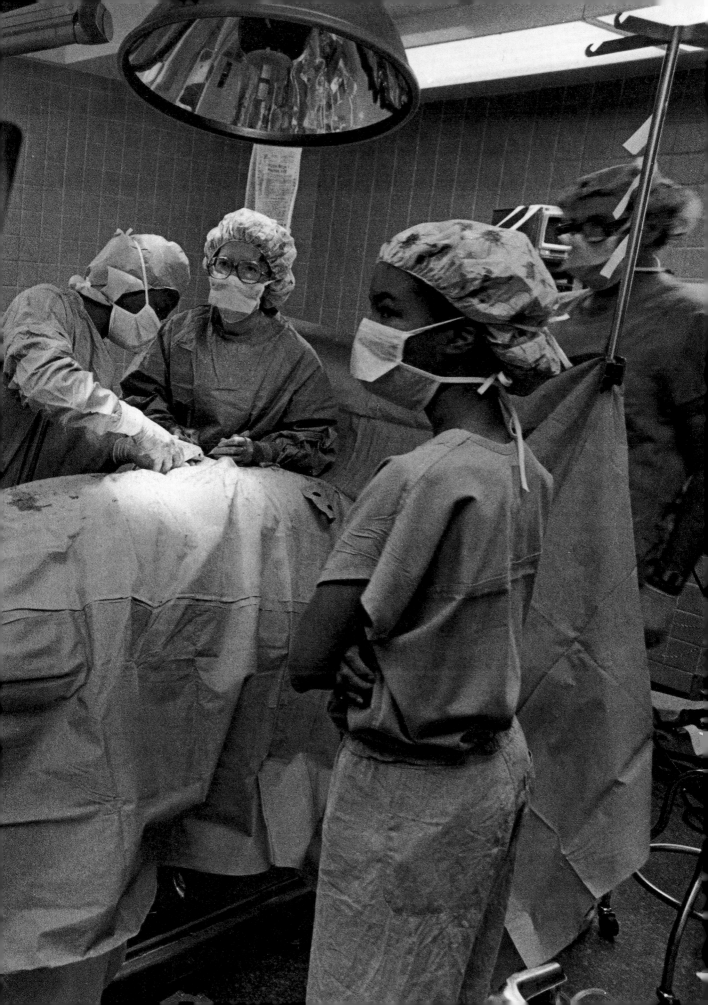

88

and white tile, the glare of huge overhead lights, monitors, a mess of wires, plastic tubes, beakers, stainless steel tables. What they call the heart of the hospital is such an undersized, utilitarian place. I had hoped for a glass wall to stand behind, a stool out of the way to sit on, but there is nothing except the skinny edges of this twelve-foot-square room to hug with my shoulder blades. I'm back as far as I can get.

Suddenly, Mrs. Burke is naked. I forget to look at her breast even though I know she, too, has had a mastectomy. Her pubic area and her white belly where they will do the cutting are exposed. Her skin is relaxed.

"Can I put in a Foley tube now?" asks one of the nurses.

No one answers. The residents and students and nurses move around the patient in a constant, busy flow. "Can I put in the Foley tube now?" she asks a second time.

Someone has apparently answered yes because the nurse spreads Mrs. Burke's pale legs and paints her urethra with antiseptic. It runs across the pubis like thin menstrual blood. Dr. Kelley holds more of the antiseptic in a plastic bag. He dips a long-handled sponge into the greenish-red fluid and begins to baste Mrs. Burke's torso from her chest bone to her pubic bone.

Mrs. Burke had been frantic last night. The mother of five children, two of them sick with cystic fibrosis, she was anxious to get back home, to get well again, so she can care for them. She had not been able to eat any supper before coming into the hospital. So while we talked, a beautiful black aide wearing plum lipstick and elegant high heels brought her a sandwich, an orange, and a carton of milk.

Yes, she had had her left breast removed eight years ago, she said, pressing against her nightgown with one hand. Then adjuvant chemotherapy had made her so ill that her doctor continued to treat her with only one of the anti-cancer drugs. Now cancer was back—in her bones this time. So she was scheduled for a hysterectomy, the cutting away of her ovaries, to stem the monthly flow of estrogen that could accelerate the bone cancer. "Dr. Deckers said there might also be something suspicious about my liver," she said, looking up into my face. "He's going to check on that, too."

Deckers is late. They are all waiting for him—nurses, Dr. Kelley, students, the anesthesiologist. Finally he strides in, huge, mumbling behind his mask. His wet arms are stretched before him like the lead actor in a thousand Hollywood hospital dramas. The scene is so corny I almost lose my nervousness.

"I have four medical students. Why do they give them to me?" he asks loudly in mock anger. "Four medical students! That's like getting four hemorrhoids. No one gets four hemorrhoids at once." Everyone laughs, even the medical students. Even Gene.

Dr. Deckers twirls and twists into a sterile paper coat and pushes his hands into thin rubber gloves. One after another, the doctors spin into their work clothes in a kind of ritual dance and move to the table.

"I kept saying 'Oh, God. Oh, God.' The mask was put on my face and I was drifting, drifting, up into the clouds, floating around up there. And I was trying to hold onto my daughter. My daughter was drifting, drifting, and drifting away. Made me feel like I died. I grabbed for her. I grabbed her hand, someone's hand, squeezing it, not wanting to let it go. Must have been a doctor's hand.

"I got hold of my daughter, pulling her back to me. God, Oh, God. Oh, God. Pulling her back. Got you. Just as I got her back I woke up, and I was crying . . . No, I couldn't hear nothing, and I couldn't feel any pain, till after I came out of it. All I was thinking about was my daughter."

I am staring at Mrs. Boles. Industrial-size staples close the ten-inch incision in her belly and tubes hang from her nose and her arm. But there she is, in Recovery the day after surgery, talking excitedly, even smiling. I smile back. I am coming to like her, though to be honest, when we first met, she seemed so thoughtlessly alive. All those soap operas and leaving everything to her doctors, dodging and fending off the truths of her cancer. I hadn't realized how essentially alone she was with her illness.

"I was telling Dr. Feller all about it last night, but he was too busy. You know I'd put my life in his hands any day. He is just like God to me. And I told Gene when he visited this morning and my cousin. It was her only visit here, and she couldn't get over what's happening to me. They will all probably tell everyone they know about it, about my experience up in heaven. I think it was heaven. It had to be heaven . . .

"Tomorrow. I don't know what it will be like tomorrow. The safe dreams I suppose. So long as it's safe dreams, I don't mind. Of course, if I have it, I have it. My daughter asked, 'Why did they have to cut you? Did they have to do that to you?' And all I could say was that in due time, things happen."

Walking through the cancer ward I hear a name being whispered. Mary Tobler. Room 551. I stop, for I remember her from last week—a big woman with a grim, gray face, able to hear but refusing to communicate. The medical students ignore me and go on talking softly about removing the hyperalimentation needle, the thin tube through which Mary Tobler receives her food.

We begin morning rounds with pretty Mrs. Kayes, who is going home today—oh, happiness—although she still carries tumors in her neck and pelvis. Upcoming chemotherapy treatments may arrest them. She had been upset about losing her hair to the anticancer drugs. Today she looks healthy and very happy.

"The pain in your neck will get better soon following a last dose of radiation," Dr. Kelley tells her.

"It's not a pain, more like a pressure, as if someone were standing back there squeezing my neck."

"No one back there," Kelley says laughing and peering playfully over her shoulder.

Mr. MacDonald in 528 asks Gene why anyone who didn't have to would want to experience cancer. "Pictures," he says, "are such baloney." But as Gene is leaving the room, Mr. MacDonald grabs his hand, "Please just tell everyone I'm hanging in here."

Mr. Farley and Mr. Killison, in the adjoining room, are both heavy smokers. Farley is a three-pack-a-day man, his breathing blurred with mucus. I have to hold my breath listening to his struggle for air. He says he doesn't want to be forced to cough.

"You'll drown," Dr. Kelley tells him.

And Mr. Killison is still angry, although not quite as furious as he was last week when he told Dr. Kelley he had had enough and was sick and tired of people poking at him. Kelley keeps trying to talk to him and touches his shoulder where the Johnny opens, revealing dry, white skin. Old skin. But Mr. Killison's anger seems to be the only defense he has left. Perhaps, he is not used to being dependent on other people. If so, what a lousy disease to get. Cancer of the stomach, gastrointestinal CA, as the students blithely say. Not a disease to be alone with.

Leon Doucette is weaker than when we saw him last week, very much sicker than the first time I met him. Cancer of the liver has forced his body to retain fluids and poisons. He has swelled like a caricature of a fat man—a small face with blackish eye sockets balanced above a huge stomach on a neck delicate as a flower stamen.

"We're going to begin taking that swelling down," Kelley says, touching Mr. Doucette's belly. He has been promising relief for two weeks, since I first began to accompany the staff on rounds. This time he speaks of pricking the bubble of air to collapse the swelling. It sounds impossible to me, a child's idea of treatment—like letting the air out of a balloon.

But Mr. Doucette says, "Okay, doc," nodding, and looking up into Dr. Kelley's face as if this were the first time the matter had been broached. "Okay, next week, after radiation gets through with me."

"Hello, how are you? Good-bye," to one face after another, as if we are on a stroll through a factory of symptoms and pains. I am feeling blistered, useless, not able to say or do a damn thing that is an ounce of help. But to patients, rounds are the most important part of each day, for it is then that they are the centers of attention and the experts on their disease.

Dr. Kelley works from room to room with a soothing efficiency, and the students follow along, although they do not always share his interest in each case. The resident, Dr. Sills, whom patients call the foreign doctor because of his Indian accent, often detaches himself from the business of rounds and distractedly turns over a patient's newspaper here, a book's pages there. Sometimes all of us—doctors, students, reporters, and patients—stop conferring in deference to the shadows and bold light of the ubiquitous television on the wall. The make-believe of game shows and soap operas cuts across the cancer ward.

Mrs. Benefito is asleep, a tube held in place with a square of adhesive extending from her nose. Her hair is combed perfectly; her small hands, tiny really, with a wedding ring on the left one, hold a pillow to her stomach where the colostomy incision was made a few days ago. The doctors don't bother to wake her.

Suddenly, there is a terrible sound in the corridor, a quick gasping as if someone cannot get enough breath. It gets louder. A sob for air, in and out. Someone is in distress, but no one runs to help.

"Mary Tobler" reads the patient's chart outside the door. At first, I think she is having a seizure, her arms and legs twitch spasmodically on the blanket, jerking up and down. Her eyes are open in a head that is stretched on a stiff neck, but she is not awake. A coma?

"Then there is nothing to be done," the students say turning away to continue rounds. Dr. Kelley leaves to telephone Mrs. Tobler's relatives. It seems as if someone should stay with her. Her body is still trying hard, trying to pump out the poisons. I feel frightened and awkward. I am seeing terrible, private things and don't want to stay either.

The students, gathered at the nurses' station, are talking to chief surgeons Mozden and Deckers about two cases scheduled for presentation today. Dr. Sills will discuss Mrs. Benefito, whose colostomy and previous radiation have caused a fusion of tissues in her vagina. At first, she and her husband tried to make love to keep the area open as Dr. Deckers suggested, but it wasn't possible. No wonder Mrs. Benefito has a compulsion to always look pretty, no wonder she is refusing chemotherapy for fear of losing her hair. She is only forty-six, but she might never again feel a man inside her body.

Two women and a man pass us carrying chairs into Mrs. Tobler's room. Her family, I suppose. Forty to fifty-year-old people, but they look like children. They look stunned, as if they have just been awakened unexpectedly.

The rounds wind down. Natasha, a student, is making a stab at describing a case, but Dr. Feller takes over and begins to talk about an upcoming operation. He is unshaven, tired; his arm in his white smock rests against mine for a few minutes. I hear Mary Tobler at the end of the corridor, her gasps loud and fast, but I feel warm, companionable here.

"Dr. Kelley, Dr. Kelley? Can you do something?"

It is Mrs. Tobler's daughter, pale and shaking, her mouth twisted with tears. The terrible gasping has stopped. Kelley follows her back into the room. He draws the curtains around the bed, enclosing Mrs. Tobler and her relatives, separating them from any niggling hospital life that might interfere.

"They know there isn't anything I can do," Kelley says to me later. "But they need to have the doctor there; they have to do something. I talk to them so they can turn the experience around a little, so it becomes positive."

"I tell them it is a privilege for them to be there, for them to be able to share their mother's death. It is a privilege not many people have."

He is looking straight at me. I can't hold back my tears.

"And it's true," he says. "It's true."

The gold chain at my throat makes me feel especially naked. I touch the links, imagining them glittering against my brown skin, although my color is really the result of only a couple of hours of sun. More red than brown. Everyone else at the lake wears clothes, even Gene, who jumps in in his jockey shorts. On the dark beach are little boys of eleven and twelve, their hair smeared across their heads from the force of their dives, and a young couple wrapped in a towel kissing.

As I step out of my clothing, I step back from Mrs. Tobler and the whole mournful week. I am swallowed up by the black water, knees first, thighs, belly, breast, face. Without my glasses I can see very little—the float, a darker square on the water's surface, and the moon, of course, veined and swollen, palpitating in the heat left over from the day. This isn't a suburban lake to me but Africa, the way Africa appears in my dreams—hazy with heat and illimitable life.

"Is that you?" I call out.

I reach backwards with my foot, toes recoiling from soft weeds, and touch a firm, alien shape. It is Gene.

"You scared me," I say to what I can see of his face, dark eye holes with lake water running off his forehead.

> B528 Leon Doucette "Still sounding better then he looks."
> Mrs. Ziff, F328 Late 20's Acute leukemia.
> Grace Kelly 527 Breast cancer metastasized to lung.

Wednesday morning, and we're back on rounds. I scratch down a few notes as we move along the hallway. In our week's absence from C-5, Mr. Andrews has lost another ten pounds; he's lost eighty in the last few months. Mrs. St. Croix is being readied for a "middle-sized" operation. Lillian Canning's going home. Mr. Farley will receive double doses of radiation, then go home next week. Radiation is being used to shrink Sally Powers's brain tumor and to restore her eyesight. Mrs. Powers's roommate Mary Storelli has died.

"I looked up into the blue sky," says Sally Powers settling back against her pillow. "I was going to make some coffee to celebrate the blue sky, but as I went by the curtain of Mary's bed I sensed that something was wrong. I went to get the doctors, and they said she had been in great pain and was gone. There was nothing to say, so I went back to the room and sent a little prayer out the window to that beautiful sky. If you take a picture, please include that bed as a sign of respect for her being gone."

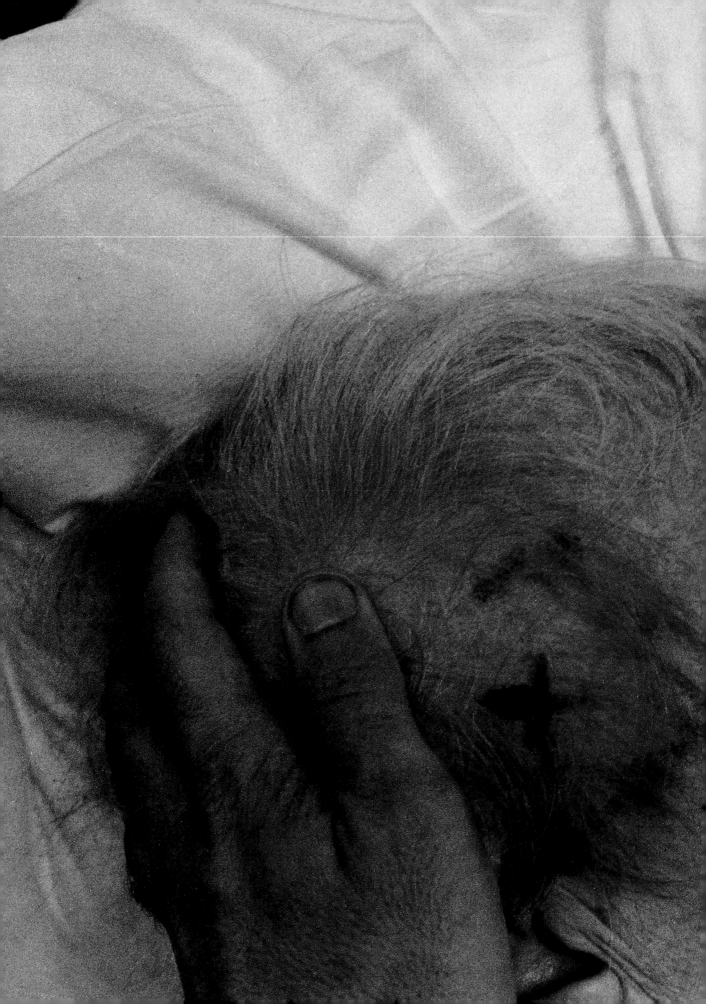

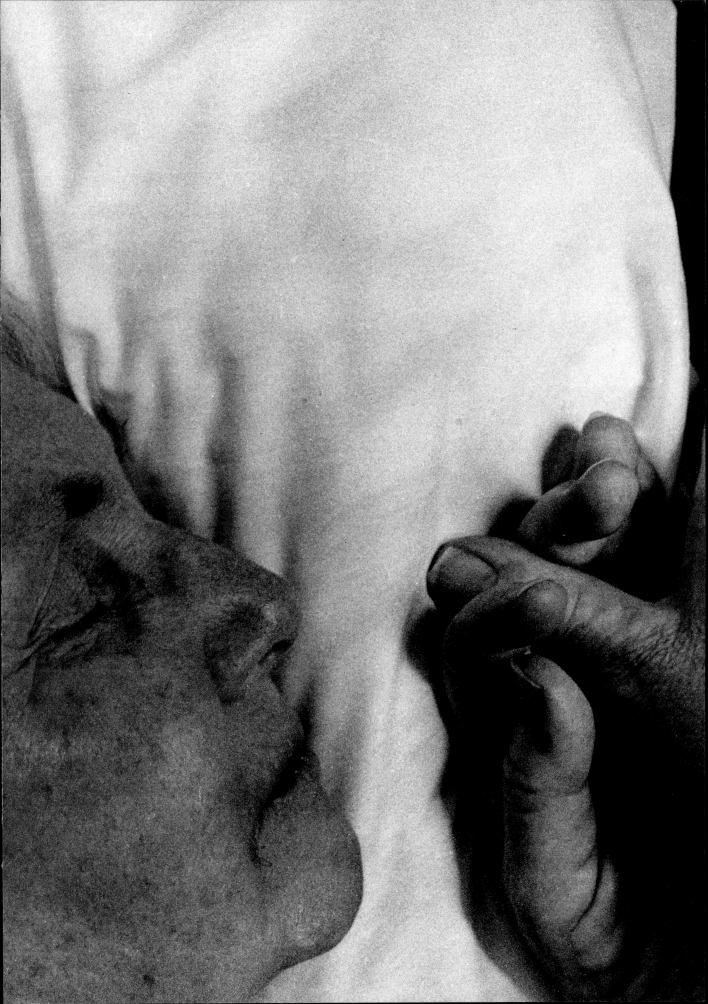

Gene kisses her forehead, then without talking, trails his fingers from her eyelids to her cheeks, beneath her thinning hair to the radiation mark, the purple target there against her skull.

"They don't use the word cobalt," she says to him. "That's the word I'm frightened of. Any treatment that's necessary is okay with me as long as it isn't called cobalt. Do you know the color of cobalt? Cold blue, an icy color. But even now, closing my eyes and thinking of it, I feel hot, I'm burning up. I am a side of beef that is being roasted.

"After the mastectomy I had radiation four times a week for five weeks and was scared to death each time—even though I had been told by the staff what to expect. The size of the machinery scared me—the Betatron as big as this room coming down right over me.

"My mastectomy? You wouldn't believe how many of my friends have had mastectomies. And it always seems to be the left breast. The first time you change that dressing, ah, the horror. I thought my body was desecrated, after I took such good care of it. But it's just a cut, not your whole life. Of course if you're young the loss could mean a great deal more than it has to me.

"Being in a bathing suit, my scar, nothing bothers me now, except that people won't talk about my having cancer, like they won't call me old. Senior citizen or golden ager, but never old, which is what I am. I am old. Now don't get me wrong, people are kind to you when you have cancer. They want to do everything but breath for you, but the misconceptions continue to fly, such as the beleif that people get cancer because they don't take care of themselves. That's a lot of crap. I swim every day, exercise, and enjoy life. I have twins who are fifty, a daughter who is forty-eight and one who is forty-two. Twenty-one grandchildren. Four great-grandchildren.

"You know it's not so different from when we were kids. In Hanson, Massachusetts, there was a TB hospital. Tuberculosis was a bad disease—you wasted away to nothing. Well, back then, when I went by the place with my friends, we held our breath.

"My eyes? I woke up one morning and I couldn't see anything. It was the Fourth of July, and I was just back from being in the hospital with pneumonia. Things moved by me at first in silhouette, then I didn't see anything at all. I stayed in bed, panicked, and thought maybe I was hallucinating like when I ran 104 degree fever and had those hallucinations in the hospital. It was, of course, a tumor, a tumor on my optic nerve that was affecting my left eye. So they're irradiating the right side of my brain—a treatment a day. You get a little schedule, and you fit your life right in. I'm losing my hair, but so what? I can see again. Hallelujah! I will paint again. I even saw the CT scan of my brain, and to me it was a most beautiful abstraction.

"The future? I don't make plans too far ahead. My mother used to take three little shuffle steps just to get going in the morning. Every morning now I think of her, cause I do the same little shuffle myself."

I sneak back to Room 520 to continue my chat with Evelyn Doherty, who made me laugh out loud this morning with her snappy retorts to the medical students' endless questions. She is a peppery, chain smoking ginger-haired woman, full of bawdy stories about her long career as an obstetrical nurse.

I've been visiting her as often as I can, grateful for the fun we share, though I know that in doing so I am breaking the head social worker's rules that we involve ourselves only with Dr. Deckers's and Dr. Kelley's patients. Mrs. Doherty has a brain tumor metastasized from an earlier breast cancer and now has trouble walking. Her doctor is a neurologist whom we haven't met.

Mrs. Doherty is talking about how much she values her independence when the head social worker calls me out of the room.

"I wish you wouldn't choose Mrs. Doherty," Joan whispers, "She isn't one of Deckers's patients, and she has a brain tumor, you know. Don't you think you are being unfair? She isn't really herself anymore."

"But I like Mrs. Doherty," I protest. "I like her. We met on rounds last week and just hit it off." A second social worker and a nurse approach Gene who's been waiting in the corridor, circling him with their complaints, ". . . not in her right mind . . . tumor . . . taking advantage . . ."

I find Mrs. Doherty to be sharp-witted and functioning well, with the exception of her legs. Why shut her away from me? Because she's not the "perfect patient"? Because she's dying? Because she's so outspoken? Because she's critical of some of the care she's received? Medical personnel should dispel half-truths and suppositions about cancer, not mouth new ones.

Yesterday, Mrs. Doherty told her nurse about the first time she had chemotherapy. "Oh, my God, I was petrified. Oh, my God, what's happening to me. This is a teaching hospital, with lots and lots of people on the job. Why the hell didn't you or someone make sure I knew what was going to happen to me?"

Joan reminds me, again, that I agreed to work through the social services department, and says that if I continue to interview unauthorized patients, I will jeopardize our project. Angry and embarrassed, I walk away. I walk past Mrs. Doherty's door trying to find the words to explain why I can no longer visit her. But there is no sensible way to interpret the hospital's rules, and I cannot tell her that the nurses think she is mentally impaired. I pass back and forth in front of the room four times, five times, six, knowing she must be waiting for me. Mrs. Doherty is scheduled to be released soon, in two or three days. I tell myself it will be a lot smarter if I get her telephone number and call her at home. Under my breath, I wish her good fortune and good-bye.

Mary Gallante is remembering for me back to the birth of her children. Sliding through the years to her wedding day. Back to her childhood. She looks exhausted, overwhelmed. The tumor board's decision is to curtail further treatment of her advancing lung cancer. When she is not surrounded by people, she stares at the floor or out the window at the sky.

Mrs. Gallante is from an old school Italian family. The relatives who arrive toward evening for her birthday celebration are upset that Gene and I are in the room to see her depressed like this.

"Don't let them take your picture," her sister tells her.

Mrs. Gallante presses her lips together. "It's my life," she says. "I say, yes."

FOUR

Why do I do this? Drive after work at the *Ledger* up and down the devastated, disappearing Dorchester Streets. Magnolia, Bird, Quincefield. Lasalle's Bar on Dudley is boarded up. Gone, too, is the "five-and-dime" and our old green three-decker house on Humphrey Street. Number Eighteen. Our walk-through apartment on the second floor had a shaky back porch on which we partied and danced with our friends. But that was six or seven years ago.

At 11:30 p.m. the storefronts and windows at Uphams Corner are dark and there are just a few cars, so the traffic lights blink only obscure warnings, not what daylight traffic demands. It is as if everyone and everything is gone, leaving just memories. I pull to the side of the street and turn the car motor off.

It was about nine months ago that the letter came from the Boston Hospital for Women telling me the admission dates for my biopsy. A little booklet, *Caring for the Surgical Patient*, instructed me to bring a robe, slippers, and something to read, like I was going on a cruise. Gene read the letter and said, "Let's go for a drink."

On the way to the Victoria we drove through Uphams Corner, where a young boy was running with his Irish Setter. The dog's fur lifted and settled, throwing off sparks of sunlight. Cigarette smoke drifting from the window of the car ahead twisted like musical notes in the air. People waited for buses, hurried by with groceries and babies in their arms, shouted directions to the expressway, or blew their car horns.

"You're looking at this place like you'll never see it again," Gene said to me, smiling at my tears.

It's midnight. I tool along Stoughton Street, headlights pulling one thing after another in my path—the rear ends of smashed cars, a boy on a bike, two men swaying from a barroom. A woman sits like a monument in a white nightgown on the front stoop of her rooming house. Even driving fast I can recognize Eileen, for no one else is so huge. My dear, brooding friend managed somehow to visit me almost every day I was in the hospital.

I slow down the car and wave my hand, but Eileen stares straight ahead, lost in her thoughts. I wonder if she will sit outside all night. It is the first of September, one of the last of the heatstruck summer nights.

"It's probably just a back pain," Dr. Shirely reassures me when I tell him my back hurts. "Just to be on the safe side, we'll do a bone scan." I press one side of my face, then the other, to the machine. I know as well as he does that breast cancer generally metastacizes to bone. Neither of us mentions that.

Jesus, maybe I'm a certified hypochondriac. When I found the lump in my vagina, I told Gene I didn't want to live without my private parts, without having sex. It turned out that my ovaries were screwed up from chemotherapy. There was no lump.

Even though Dr. Shirley was right after all about my back, I am still a little down. Gene wants to celebrate. Still, I am depressed that the rest of my life will be filled with these ripples of fear. The menacing machine. False alarms.

After a night of partying with friends at a photography gallery, it takes all my strength to crawl out of bed. But Gene, gobbling aspirins for his headache, insists that we get back over to C-5 to find out how Anna Gavone is doing after her surgery. I'm tired. I would telephone the hospital for information on her condition, but I feel how strong, how confoundedly strong, is Gene's desire now to see things for himself.

Mrs. Gavone is a 260-pound woman with silky white hair; yet covered with sheets and lying in the protective tangle of tubes and wires, she's hard to distinguish from the other patients in the recovery room. We double check the name on the chart, then settle down by her bed, listening to her coughing, the beeps on the monitor, and her breathing. The sound of Mrs. Gavone's breathing is the sound of waiting.

Sitting, waiting, Gene and I soon begin to behave like kids. We argue which one of the floor nurses has the best behind, and take each other's pulse and blood pressure. I squirm and giggle when Gene runs his fingers up and down the soft

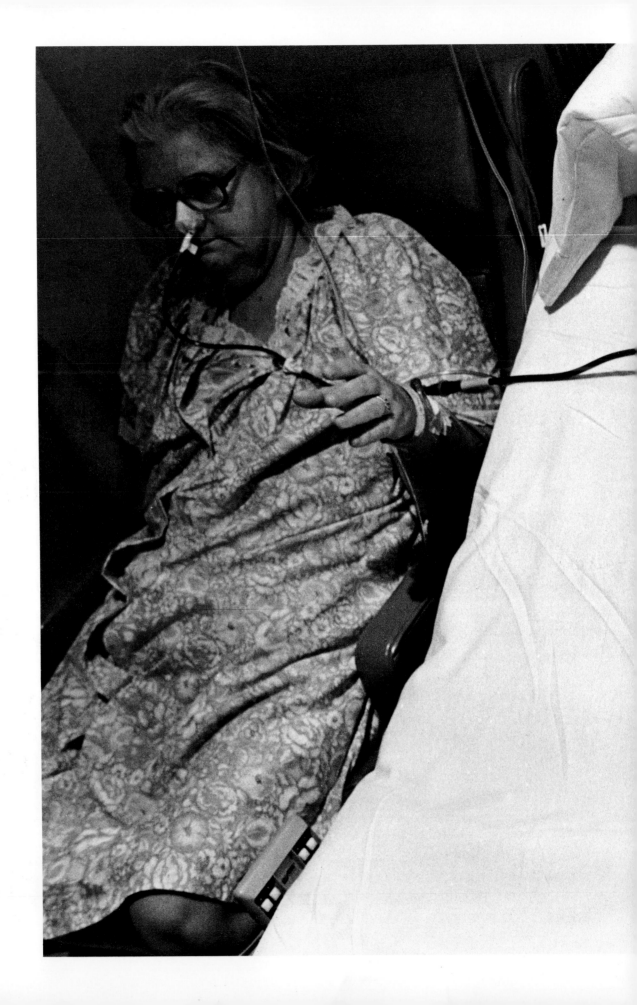

inside of my arm in search of an elusive heartbeat. We tease and make funny faces at each other, for much the same reason, I suppose, that medical students joke amongst themselves—to hold back the frightening realities.

At noon, on a sweep through the ward, Dr. Deckers stops by to make sure we're aware that Mrs. Gavone's operation has gone as planned. He describes the surgery so confidently that one might imagine he had cut her toenails, not her stomach. Then, all work and wild energy, he moves on, students in tow, while Gene and I sit.

Two hours pass. In front of me in the recovery room the patients, bristling with tubes, float on their beds like pigeons on the ocean, displaced. Hearing them wheeze for air, I think of the wind in the trees, then of a black night in Maine, in Manomet, when I was ten years old. There wasn't a moon or stars or a light on the road. My sister Moira and I lay down on our backs in the suffocating darkness, as if we were buried alive in the sky.

I catch my lower lip with my teeth to keep back the tears, and Gene mistakes my grimace for boredom. "Both Mrs. Gavone's mother and father died of cancer," he whispers in my ear. "Her father after being cared for at home; her mother the day after she first went to a doctor. The woman had concealed her symptoms and her pain for close to two years, not wanting to be another burden to the family."

When Anna Gavone's eyes open, Gene is standing by her bed. Through the thickness of the drugs she somehow recognizes him. Dizzy and nauseous though she must be, she raises her hand and forms her thumb and forefinger into the letter "o" for okay, so that he won't worry, so we can share her coming back.

"Oh, I'm to be a star," says Mrs. Gavone, pulling open her hospital gown, so that the doctors and her daughter, Susan, and her granddaughter, Kimberly, can see the incision. Kimberly, who had begged to stay during the examination, looks down at the fleshy wound and begins to breathe like she might swallow up all the air in the room. But she doesn't back away, and in a minute her panic fades. When the doctors say good-bye, Mrs. Gavone, with Kimberly beside her on the bed, talks of what brought her to C-5.

"It was twenty years ago that I began to have terrific pains and to pass blood. My family doctor couldn't figure out what was wrong with me, so he sent me to the hospital. There the doctors found a lump. A surgeon said it was a growth in the bowel. My father died of cancer of the bowel. So I went through four and a half hours of surgery, after which the doctors said, 'No, not cancer. We got everything.'

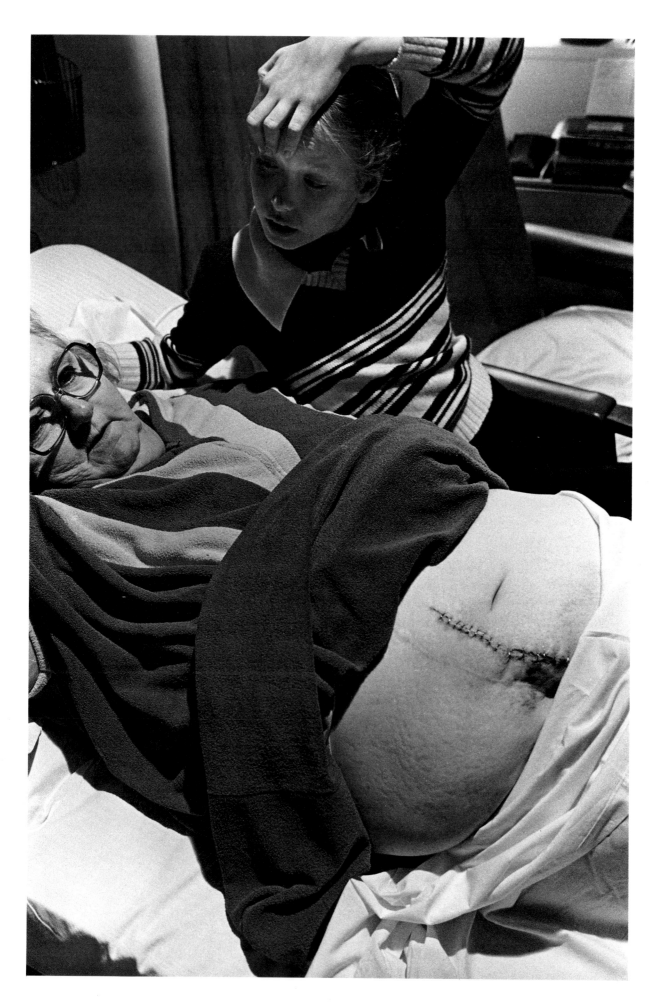

Even my family physician assured me it wasn't cancer. What I didn't know, what I couldn't know, was that my husband had told the doctors I was the kind of woman who couldn't handle bad news—so they didn't tell me.

"What I was was a dull housewife who lived in a small world—overweight, diabetic, on weight-loss medication. My husband, though, was a very social man who loved partying and his career. He was away for months on end running summer camps for a living. He didn't want me to go outside the home to work, so I didn't. I was his wife, raising his children, running his home. And he didn't tell me.

"He should have told me. Knowing would have changed the way I lived. I would have lost weight. I'm down now from 304 pounds. I would have gotten more exams. He should have told me, at least after we were divorced. No, it probably wouldn't have kept the cancer from reoccuring, I don't think, but I would have been alerted."

Mrs. Gavone turns on her side in the bed, her face reddening. She is silent for a few minutes. "God, people have to be careful. When I told my doctor a few months ago I was hemorrhaging, he told me not to worry. Since I had no pain, it must be my age. I was bleeding like I was in diapers, but again and again when I called he said, 'Don't worry! You're in the change. Age fifty-five.' When my daughter Susan found out about the bleeding, she pushed me to see my old surgeon, who gave me a D & C. Still, I went seeking the advice of a specialist. And Deckers told me it was cancer, a liver tumor. I learned also what had been written on my old medical records. 'Do not reveal cancer to patient.'"

The Dorchester light at five o'clock is faded, blurred now with windblown bits of leaves and pollen. I hang out a wash. The girl next door comes out on her back porch to take down her clothes, snapping them free of lint, and she isn't a girl at all. She's the mother of a red-haired toddler, and yes, the world is turning faster and faster. Mrs. Burke went home to her family two days ago, and Clistee Boles left the hospital yesterday morning. Gene says that no one on C-5 seemed to notice that Mrs. Boles was gone. Attendants changed the sheets and another patient, scheduled for surgery, was settled in the bed.

I put dinner in the oven and begin to do my daily exercises, feeling a little lost, cut off. Oh, I can visit Mrs. Boles and Mrs. Burke at their homes, but not for a while. The women are returning from where they had been taken care of to the reality of housework and children. This isn't the time for them to dwell on the past.

Gene's not much fun tonight. He's engrossed in the Sunday newspaper, reading three separate articles at once. The first is a report on United States covert aid to white Rhodesia; the second has Henry Kissinger announcing his sympathy for the struggle of black Rhodesians; the third names the annual winner of the Wellesley College hoop-rolling contest. If I weren't doing leg raises Gene probably would thrust the newspaper in front of me, exclaiming, "What a world!"

Day after day he reads to me, hoping to make me more aware of the larger world, explaining how international issues sift down to local levels and, in the end, affect even my most personal concerns. Revolution, civil rights, equal rights, patient's rights. But mostly, I only half listen to him, distracted from my cooking, my reading, and my own thoughts.

Gene begins to read aloud about a nursing home in Roxbury where patients were found strapped to their beds watching a broken TV. In mid-sentence, he stops, and looks straight at me. "I wouldn't mind getting older," he says, "if I wouldn't someday end up like that, all alone." Nervously he runs his fingers through his thinning hair. "Or if we had something to show for the years. Wouldn't it be nice to have a car that was paid for, or a little house with space for your dream garden? Not two beat-up cameras and thirty bucks in the bank."

Gene's vision of growing old, his whisper of losing me, is followed by a rush of angry words about tomorrow when he will again have to wrestle the bureaucracy on the cancer ward. "Doors slammed in our face by people who can only say no. No, don't take that patient's picture, or that patient's picture. No, I don't want to see what things look like or are like."

To quiet Gene I half-jokingly call him an old grouch, then kiss him. In silence he breaks down the camera he'll use tomorrow in surgery, dusts the mirror and the lens, and carefully loads the film.

The circulating nurse gives me a longsleeved coat to ward off the chill. Behind the sterile mask my breath collects and steams up my glasses. The viewfinder of Gene's camera clouds over when he puts it to his eye. The thermostat reads sixty-one degrees.

More than fifty pairs of metal clamps are lined up precisely on the scrub nurse's tray. Retractors gleam to one side, flanked by sutures and the silvery scalpels that, when drawn across the skin, will open the body. On the table, naked, being

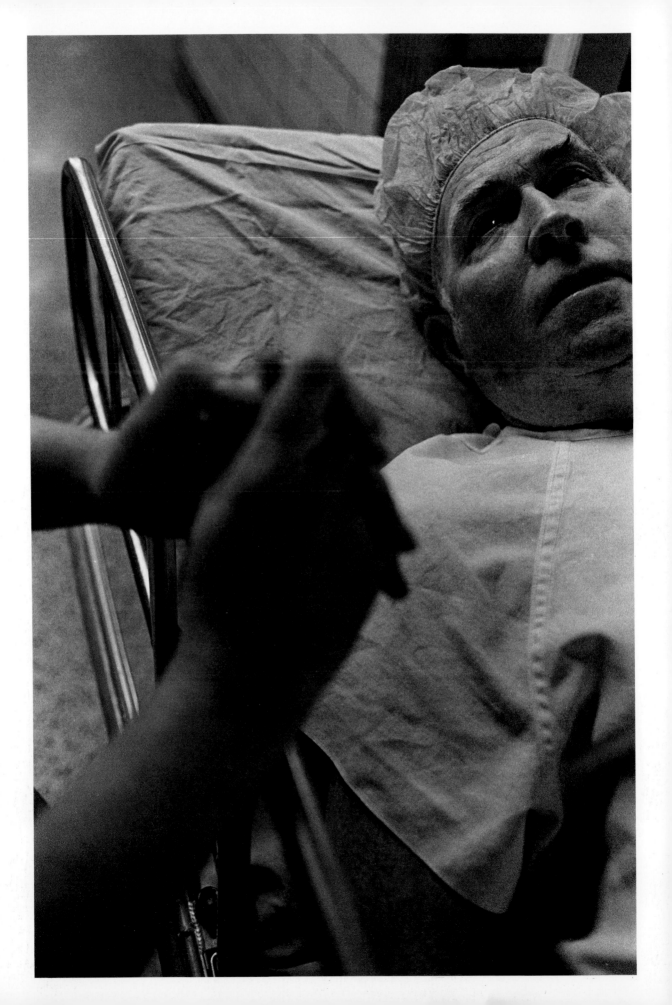

swabbed with antiseptic and poked with needles, is a middle-aged furniture mover, Martin Hayes.

Just before he was wheeled into the operating room, I stole a few minutes with Mr. Hayes, who seemed unruffled by the latest chapter of his ordeal with cancer. He told me matter of factly, "The tumor is in the bowel." But his voice shook when he spoke of his wife. "Oh, she knows me. Mary knew it was no little thing. I was bleeding, but figured it was only hemorrhoids, for I never lost a day of work in sixteen, seventeen years. Not lost a day, not a day." Mr. Hayes grasped my hand, not wanting to talk too much more about his life. "Here I am," he said. "This is me. Now, please, what about you?"

In the O.R. there is a hush. Speech is slowing down. I don't feel good. I feel foggy, far away, as if I've breathed in some of the anesthesia. "Are you sleepy yet, Mr. Hayes?" Doctor Coughlin, waiting for the sodium pentathol to take effect, absent-mindedly rubs Mr. Hayes's leg beneath the surgical drapes. "What a warm body," she says.

I wish Mr. Hayes would awaken, pull the tape from his eyelids, and get down from the operating table. Suddenly, I'm scared for him. Cancer kills so many. I smell ether and want to run from the O.R. and hide my face in my hands, but that won't change the facts. Surgery's not going to be postponed because a journalist is having an anxiety attack.

The door swings open and Dr. Deckers comes forward with his hands outstretched to receive the pale yellow gloves.

"Cancer of the rectum."

"Right angle bowel clamp. End-to-end anastomosis."

"A biological principle—tumors don't metastasize upwards."

I'm breathing deeply and slowly now, the way Dr. Shirley taught me months ago, and my mind is clearing. The voices I hear now mean business.

"Pelvis tilt no more than ten inches."

"O R positive."

"Just bisected the sigmoid colon."

From where I stand, at the rear of the table, the incision in Mr. Hayes's stomach looks like a mouth with the doctors running their fingers along its edges, then plunging in to find the cancer. Water and flecks of blood dance up the suction tube.

"Sutures in, clamps off."

"Size the bowel."

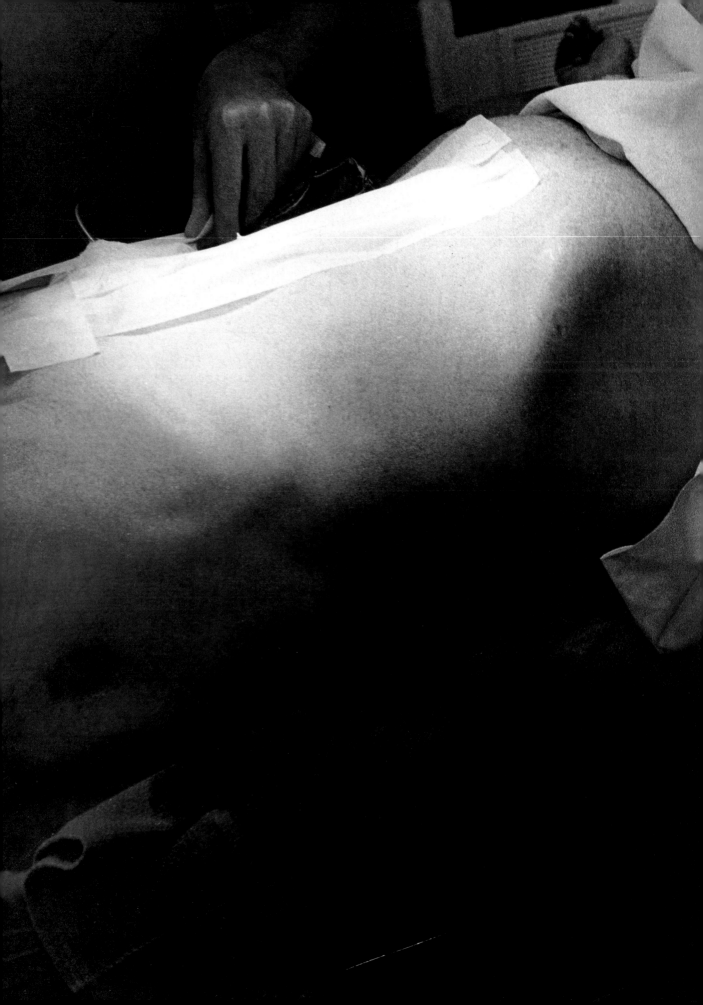

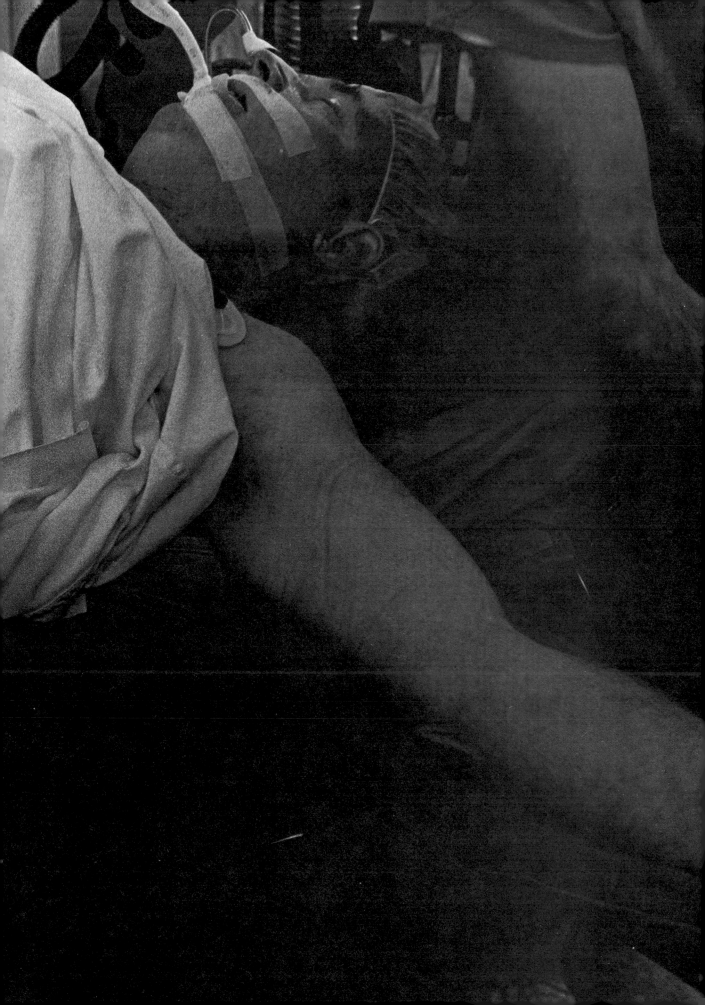

An hour later, the pressure's off. The incision is being closed and the bloody cloths, which seemed as much Mr. Hayes as his skin, are being cleared away. Dr. Deckers asks us if we would like to look closer at the section of bowel that was removed.

"Here it is."

A gray-pink chunk of flesh is dropped on a piece of plastic wrap, into my hand. It's totally unexpected. I shiver, and Gene shakes his head, but I want to see it, to study it. Surgery is relentless, redemptive. The length of bowel I'm holding is something holy.

It's only noontime, but Gene and I are fatigued and in need of quiet. Nothing prepares us for a second surgery.

"All I expect from this," whispers Mrs. Anderson, "is the truth." Nurses take her blood pressure, temperature, and pulse. An IV is started, and she is wheeled, looking stately, through the cold and sticky metal doors.

"In women of this advanced age group, we're pretty certain it's malignant," someone offers.

Dr. Deckers slices just beneath Mrs. Anderson's left nipple. Clamp, suture, cauterize. And suddenly there it is, the growth. Yellowed, a little bloody, like a piece of chicken fat. He hands it carefully to Ellie, the scrub nurse, to be packed in ice and rushed to pathology. The interns close the cut, purple sutures join the layers of fat, staples close the outer skin incision.

We all wait for the results.

In the recovery room Dr. Kelley checks Mrs. Anderson's chart, noting medications and medical history. A young resident checks the bandage and her rate of respiration, turning from time to time to the clock on the wall. "How long," I ask her, "can it take?"

Dr. Kelley leans over Mrs. Anderson and takes her hand. She coughs behind the oxygen mask, still unable to open her eyes. "You're not going to remember this," he says, "so we'll just tell you again when you wake up. It looks like everything's okay. There's no malignancy, Mrs. Anderson. Everything's okay."

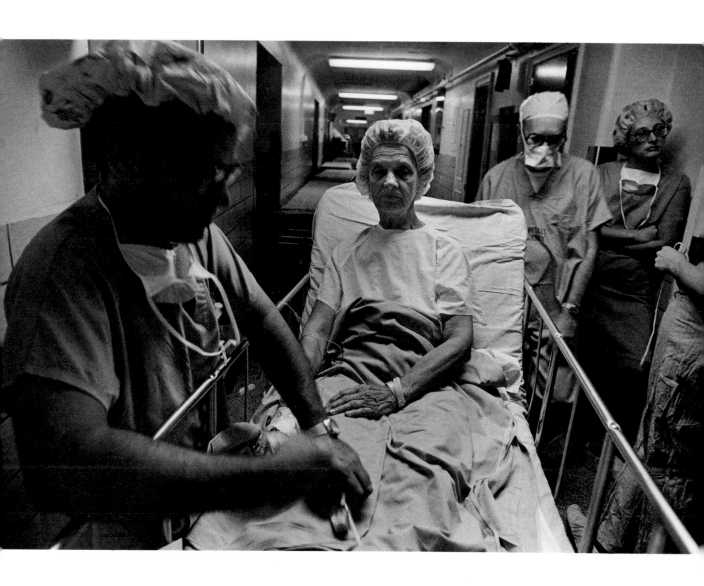

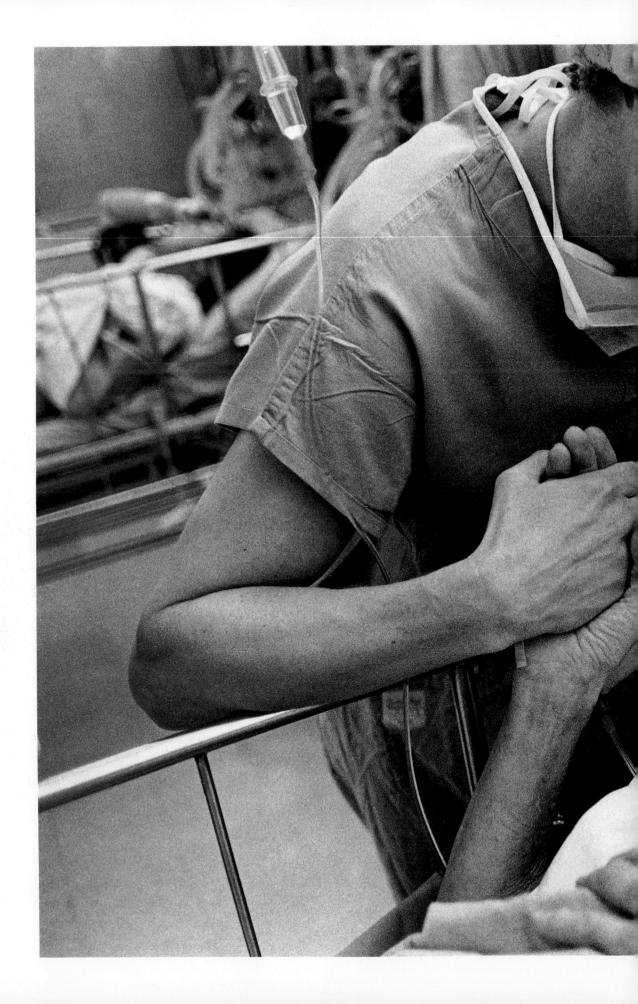

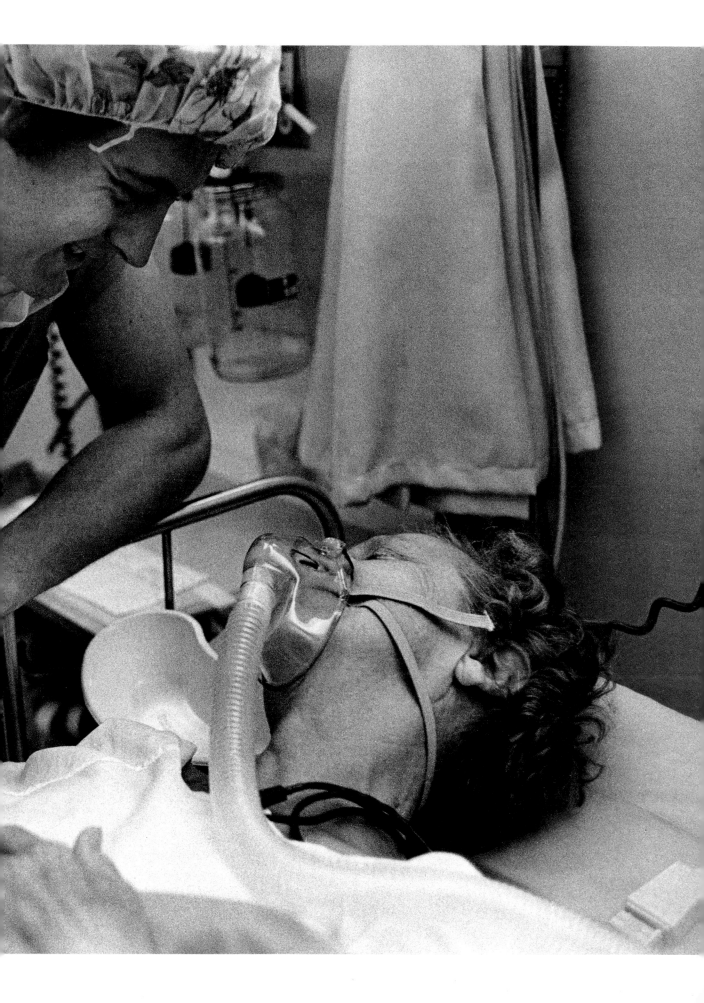

FIVE

In his sleep Gene must be reliving yesterday's surgery. He moves constantly, feet tangling in the sheets, hands twitching on the top blanket. A garbage truck moving down Chase Street awakens him before the alarm. Squeezing his face against the window he looks up between the buildings and says, "Bright blue sky."

His overnight bag is packed, and a cab's waiting. It's great he's got an assignment, but I want him to be with me in bed for a few hours more, maybe all day, until the pleasure sucks up the stresses of the past week. He's off to New York and there's nothing I can do about it. Not wanting to think about patients or problems at the hospital, I curl up in bed with the cats and turn on the radio to an old timer's station that's playing one of my father's favorite tunes. I still don't know the name of it—a lazy, sentimental song—but I remember his singing it to my mother when I was very young. He would croon, and she would join in. If she made fun of his voice, he would rush up and poke her in the ribs, making her giggle. Finally, under his merciless tickling, she would scream, "Oh, don't Bill!" Or, still singing, he would take me into his arms, sweeping me into an exaggerated waltz. Embarrassed, awkward, intensely pleased, I mimicked my mother, "Oh, Daddy, don't!"

I heard my father whistling this same song early Saturday mornings, convinced that the joyful noise was his signal for me to awaken. "It's all right to get up now. I'd like some company." I would hurry downstairs to have him read me an animal story, to talk, to peek out the window at the squirrels and blue jays. It didn't matter what we did on these mornings. Just to be alone with him, to be the center of his attention, was all I wanted.

Growing into my teens, though, I began to slightly resent the sounds of my father getting up early on Saturdays. I wanted to stay in bed with my diary on my knees, in the quiet before my sister woke up. I wanted to check myself out in the mirror and think about boys. But my father was not to be ignored. He would whistle his song, then call out, "Get up, you lazybones. Come down and set the table. Stop dreaming your life away."

My father taught me how to build a fire by rolling up pieces of newpaper, laying the thinnest of kindling on top, waiting for it to catch before setting on the heavier logs. My father taught me how to whistle. My father ran along behind my first two-wheeler until I learned how to keep it moving upright.

He was the first man who said the word "nigger" in my presence. He taught me the constellations while we lay on our backs in the grass on the first autumn nights when the air turned chill and clear. He catered to my fears of spacemen and ghosts and witches, and I became terrified of crossing a darkened room or lying in bed alone at night. He took my poems to work and read them to his friends. He allowed me to stay up late on Saturday nights, sitting on his lap, while he watched the fights shouting, "Get up, you bum!"

My mother bought me a toy garage—with lifts that raised and lowered by a small lever—because she had always wanted a toy garage of her own. She taught me the Greek alphabet and how to read before I started school. She bought me books at Christmas: Trixie Belden, Ginny Gordon, Ray Bradbury, Louisa May Alcott. She allowed me to play with her china figurines of mandarins and geishas, moving them up and down the dining room table. She told me it served me right if I got scratched for pulling the cat's tail. She slapped me across the face once, hard, when I answered her back. She didn't say anything when I wrote my first poem. She never told me about sex, but she gave me a pad and the elastic belt onto which it hooked when she saw the blood on my underpants. Two weeks after my father died, she spent twenty-five dollars on my grammar school graduation dress, eggshell blue with net cut-outs of two butterflies across the back.

Jesus, so many people with cancer. My Uncle Charles's cancer has spread to his back. Aunt Eleanor is now at Massachusetts General Hospital with cancer of the bowel. Mrs. Rodriguez, across the street, has the crude radiation tatoos on her face and throat.

I read my newspapers and watch television documentaries. I wonder can we be doing this to ourselves? The odd, the threatening news stories still attract me: stories exposing genetic manipulation, Three-Mile Island, murder-by-cancer, the neutron bomb, and carcinogens in our water and in the air we breathe. Stories to fill up already bulging file folders. What am I looking for? What do these random threats have to do with my cancer, my life? Fifteen years of dental x-rays at Dr. Hill's; foot x-rays for Jordon Marsh kiddie shoes; prescriptions for the pill from doctors Monahan, Jordon, Sullivan, Dragonas; DDT sprays drifting over our vegetables and water in Arkansas and Indiana; a chemical dumping ground in Dorchester, close to our house; sixteen years of smoking Tareyton 100s.

Oh, to be healthy again—to have a say in my future. But how? Prayers? Write "Letters to the Editor" denouncing Pentagon policies, chemical companies, and the tobacco industry? Work for a political candidate? Give money to environmental groups? On walls and causeways and bridges around Boston are signs for the next antinuclear demonstration in Seabrook, New Hampshire: "Save our Planet," "Nukes = Cancer," "Occupy Seabrook October 6."

"Goddammit. I might have known she'd pick today to have her kid."

Gene phones me sounding tired and angry. Two weeks late, Marnie and Jeff's baby is about to be born on the eve of the Seabrook demonstration. Gene has been asked to photograph the protestors who will try to stop construction of the partly-built nuclear power plant, but he wants, just as much, to record the birth at home of his friends' baby, the first birth he has ever seen. He tells me to try to sleep. He will stay up all night photographing, then join a group of us for the dawn ride to New Hampshire.

Two friends and I pick Gene up at 4 a.m., the night of sleeplessness showing as dark circles beneath his eyes.

"What did she have? Boy or girl?"

"She didn't have anything yet. The midwife says she's hardly dilated, not even two fingers." Gene falls asleep in the back of the car. The rest of us are all charged up, full of coffee and stale donuts. The moon is setting full and white as we reach the Seabrook, New Hampshire turn-off.

It is not much of a town: two small shopping malls, a state liquor store, and DeMoules market. From Route One, the Seabrook Station nuclear power plant looks like a military installation with guard checkpoints and barbed wire. Outside the main gate, a thin line of people hold lit candles symbolizing nonviolent action. As the sun rises, we see larger groups massing in the woods and out in the windblown swamps at the edge of the ocean. Dressed like mountain men and women, they move forward carrying backpacks, gas masks, wirecutters; and plastic bags of granola.

Oh, I'm so excited and scared. My legs are shaking. My mother is probably right, "a couple months out of the hospital and you're going where?"

Gene helps me across the soggy salt marsh to join the attack on the back of the plant. White construction cranes with winking red lights rear up over our heads. Policemen in riot gear charge protestors who try to cut through the security fences. Tear gas canisters strike the ground, blossoming into choking walls of smoke. Assaults with mace and icy jets of high-powered water leave the protestors and newsmen gasping and weeping, angry and terrified. It is very difficult to run in the thick mud and the tidewaters are returning, stranding us on low ground.

Suddenly, inexplicably, the action stops. I can make out Gene stumbling towards me. Ugly, red welts from repeated sprays of mace stain his forehead, neck, and cheeks.

On the way back to Boston we stop to eat in a beachside restaurant, the mud from our shoes and clothing stains the carpet. We sit across from a wedding party, the bride in a dazzling white dress and veil. And in the background a woman singer croons, "Sunrise, sunset, quickly flow the years . . ." I wonder if Marnie has had the baby yet?

No baby all the long, long Saturday night. Marnie's bedroom is warm and full of midwives, friends, cats, hot compresses, and the click of Gene's camera. It is almost luxurious to be one of so many people, all engaged in the same age-old task of birth.

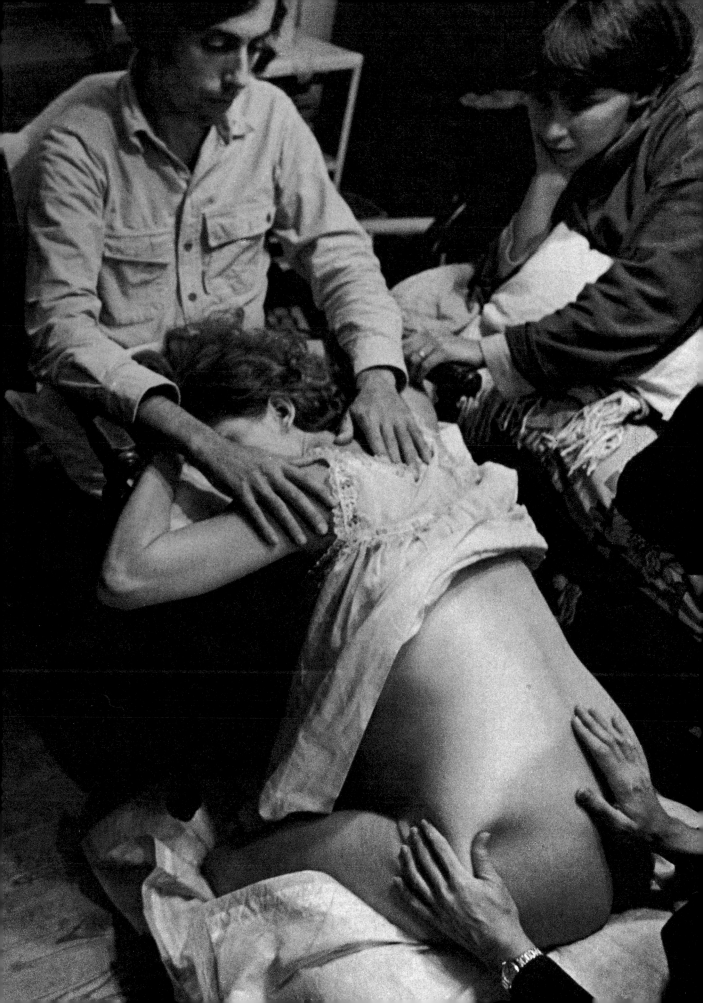

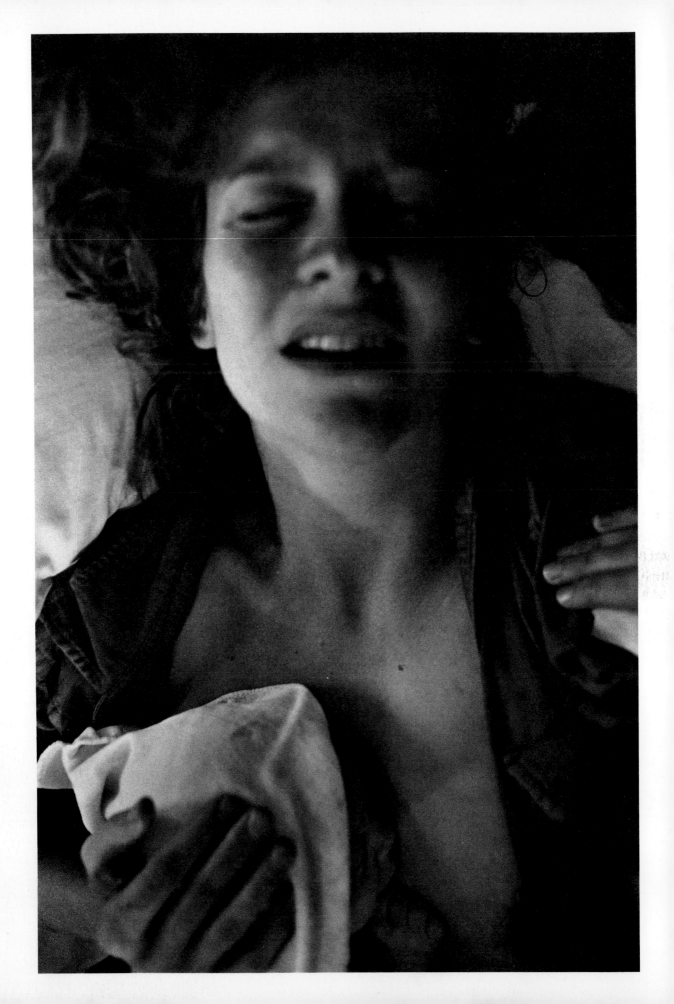

Singing at the height of her contractions, her pain tempered by a sense of purpose, Marnie is beautiful—and cared for. This is not a hospital room. There is no curtain drawn around her bed. There's no shame at her nakedness or annoyance at her demands and eccentricities. We take turns caressing Marnie's lustrous skin, the only communication she is capable of receiving, then fall asleep, one by one, in chairs, on the floor.

At 6:30 Sunday morning, Marnie begins to scream, dragging us back from dreams of shouting protestors. She yells "Come. Come, baby!"

Such a small opening. Someone is stretching the skin at the edge of the vagina where the blood bubbles. There it is. Convoluted, deep-wrinkled. The skull slips through. It is a nightmare image, a demon, an exorcism. Suddenly it is much more than that, and less. Another person is swimming over into a new life.

The Sunday after Thanksgiving. It is a year ago to the day I noticed the pain in my left breast. I think that is what's wrong with me these last few days, hyperventilating like crazy and too nervy to sleep. A year of statistics, and case histories, and raking over the coals with people who are just beginning treatment.

Talking with Martin Hayes at the hospital tonight was so difficult it made me sweat with the effort—getting the information while trying not to hurt, or pry, or be condescending, or naive, or stupid, or threatening, or mushy-emotional. "An admirable task," as nurse Linda suggests. Perhaps. But maybe not the best course for my own peace of mind and strung-out nerves. A few nights ago I thought I saw flickers of light at the edge of my eye as I was reading. It may have even been my glasses catching the reading light. Yet I immediately thought of the symptoms of a brain tumor. Indigestion, and I think of stomach cancer.

I wonder why this fear all of a sudden. Perhaps it has always been there bubbling beneath my show of confidence or, perhaps, it is my first year anniversary. American cancer statistics cite probabilities of recurrences after one, two, three, four, five years; which door is the tiger really behind? Certainly I am upset that our work is being threatened by hospital interference. What an awful thought—to let all those generous patients down.

A half hour into morning rounds Gene mutters, "What a waste of time" and drops out to get another cup of coffee. He's pissed off that we're not being introduced to the new patients on the ward or invited inside the hospital rooms. But I continue on, trailing after the doctors to learn what I can learn.

The doctors and students talk among themselves as they hurry along, and I take dreary, mechanical notes. Standing out in the hallway, all I get are glimpses of hands and faces—a very sick man trying not to look sick, a man clutching a framed photograph, a woman brushing her hair.

Each day, Gene and I are permitted to visit fewer and fewer rooms. There are almost no referrals from the social workers, no lists of incoming patients, no introductions, no access. Once we had been made to feel at home, a part of the oncology department; now we are being treated as outsiders.

There's been a turnover in the staff on C-5. The crew that befriended Gene and me when we first came onto the ward has split up. One intern is transferring to Cape Cod Hospital for further studies; another to City Hospital. The greatest loss for us is the rotation of Bill Kelley from oncology to pathology and radiology. Dr. Kelley had been our support and an inspiration. On his morning rounds, which often took hours, he would gently examine the patients, comfort the sickest, tell jokes when it was appropriate, put his arms around people when he thought it might help. Replacing him as the chief resident is the insular, unsmiling Dr. Maureen Coughlin who prides herself on conducting "lightning" rounds—"lightning" because they take so little time.

It is just before Christmas, and Gene's working in Denver. I go to Mrs. Kenney's operation, an adrenalectomy, and stand looking on. There is no camera. How useless I feel—just to be standing here taking notes:

> 1 - 2 - 3 - 4 - 5 *sponges* . . .
> *May need a little more incision* . . .
> *See this stuff here? That has to come off the ribs* . . .
> *It's fifty-two out there, and we can expect even milder weather* . . .

9:33 A.M.   200 units of blood lost . . .
You women got great fingers for this sort of thing . . .
Doctor, with gentleness, gentleness, lift it off . . .
Exercise the full expression of your womanhood . . .
Call Kelley and tell him I'm ready to go onto Mrs. Barnes.

When Dr. Deckers wacks Mrs. Kenney on the fanny—she is up in the air, asleep, of course—and says, "I hope this will do it for you, Helen," I realize I can't be doing this anymore. It is over. I am feeling superfluous, lonely for Gene, sick. The last time seeing Joan, the social worker, she told me that Mary Gallante, Leon Doucette, and Mrs. Doherty had died.

Today is the day for good-byes.

I find Kay Meyers and her son Mike at the MIT clinical experimental unit. She is wolfing down a huge Italian sandwich.

"I took off some of the onions," she tells me mischeviously, "because it's an awfully small room."

Both of us laugh, although it's hard to see how she can be relaxed. University Hospital radiates her tumors four days a week, and once a week she comes here to receive hypothermia treatments. An ultrasound machine delivers heat of about 104 degrees into the tumor. "Like a fever," one of the technicians tells me.

Five years ago Kay found the first lump in her right breast. She speaks about the doctors at a hospital in Beverly, Massachusetts who performed a biopsy under anesthesia, then a mastectomy without bothering to awaken her. She isn't angry at them. "That's just the way they did it," she says.

But her son's furious at the doctors, at the hospital, the American Cancer Society, the American Medical Association, the Federal Drug Administration. He rails against the FDA's refusal to ban cigarettes; against the Cancer Society for spending more money, he insists, on administration than on research.

The doctor arrives and bows to us. Mrs. Meyer removes her blouse and bra. I look at the red circles and small black crosses the radiologists have drawn on her side and on her chest, earmarking the tumors beneath her skin.

Even from the street, Eleanor's house in Beverly Farms smells of boiled vegetables and grains. No wonder. When Eleanor opens the door for me she is holding a bowl of brown rice, stirring it with a spoon. "Excuse me Dorothea," she says, "I've already had my lunch, but little Miss Piggy is still hungry." She has a strange way of talking, almost as if English were a second language. She clips her words neatly, sounding the t's and d's precisely, as if her teeth had grown too large for her face.

It is possible, I suppose, that one's teeth can become too big in a shrunken face. She is thin, but not as thin as she was a month ago at the macrobiotic workshop in Brookline. Back then, she was yellow, jaundiced from her failing liver, a skeleton with skin drawn over the bones.

"You look terrific," I say to her, marveling that it could be true, "a hundred times better."

"Oh, yeah? You really think so? That's good."

We discuss where we shall sit and decide on the kitchen so Eleanor can eat her rice and face me. She offers me something that sounds like bianki tea, but there is no milk or sugar to put in it. It tastes like boiled tree bark and, mercifully, it's too hot to drink.

As she tells me the story of her illness and what she calls her "recovery," she prepares our afternoon meal—something called millet burgers that are made with rice, millet, onion, and butternut squash.

"They are delicious," she assures me.

After they let me into their apartment, Pat Paris and her mother sit down and stare at each other. Neither of them asks me to be seated.

"Is there something wrong?" I ask. Then slightly anxious, "Can I help?"

"No. Not much," says Pat in a whisper. Then raising her voice, "Mother, you've got to understand why I'm acting the way I'm acting. The doctors say that I now have it in my bones."

"Oh," groans Mrs. Paris, "what's going to happen to me next?"

"Look, lady. Excuse me, lady. I'm the one who has the cancer. Although if you want it that bad, I'll be happy to give it to you."

Why do this in front of me, I wonder. Why? I see myself running back down the stairs.

"My mother thinks I'm a pain in the ass, and I am. I'm spoiled, an only child. But even so—shouldn't your mother always be in your corner? I wouldn't be surprised to find out she's already bought me a casket. She's probably paying on it right now. I don't want respect from my friends or my family after I'm dead. Why can't people take the time to share feelings with you when you are alive?"

Feeling sick, I head for the door. I want to remember Pat as the gutsy woman who curled her own hair and put on lipstick the day after her mastectomy, but she keeps on griping.

Oh, God, I'm beat, strung out like a frayed wire. A fourth good-bye today? But how can I say no? Today is Rita's last day at the hospital; she is being sprung. I can't tell her I'm exhausted—as if to say, "Thanks a lot for spilling your guts, but see you later." Is that what journalists do? Come to the end of a story and type the "30" and put away the people along with their notepads?

Rita has been waiting for me all day, with her belongings packed in a flowered tote bag. She is edgy, not very kind to the nurse. When they say good-bye and hug, the nurse is rueful and Rita looks as if she is playing a part, making me wonder how much I've really come to know her. Rita once said she had the support of a close, loving family, yet her brother and sister visited only once, briefly on a Sunday, leaving behind a gold chain with the price tag affixed. And the spectacularly beautiful daughter in California never called or wrote

I drive her to Brookline. We sit at the counter of the restaurant where she had been a waitress, but Rita doesn't drink her coffee; she is moving away from me. She barely speaks.

SIX

It has been almost two years now. Four separate scares: the sore breast last July; the imagined growth in my vagina last September; in January the persistent ache in my lower back; and this last week the pea-shaped lump on my vulva which has turned out to be a harmless cyst. All scares with happy endings.

Gene and I leave Dr. Shirley's office, our arms around each other. I do one of my happy jumps, straight up, legs bent at the knees. We leave ugly Brook House and its warren of doctors' offices behind. The sun is September sun, golden. We drive past the front door of the Boston Hospital for Women, as we have done so many times in the last two years.

"Wait, wait," I say to Gene.

A big, black moving truck is parked at the top of the circular driveway. Of course. In July I read an article in the *Boston Globe* reporting the sale of the old hospital building to a Boston contractor who proposes to make the imposing yellow brick structure over into hundreds of condominiums. The guts of the hospital—doctors, nurses, patients, records—were moved two months ago into a new structure downtown.

"Make some pictures of the hospital for me, for old time's sake."

While Gene photographs, I stand in the warm sunlight reminiscing with the moving men about that most horrible yet happiest time in my life. In turn they begin teasing us about our good feeling for the place.

We go inside with them. The long blue corridors, still painted with yellow, green, and red arrows, are eerily empty. The pharmacy is boarded up; bulletin boards are cleared of news. The young guard tells us his shift is almost up, but we won't have any problem coming back tomorrow.

"Can we go take a quick look at the rooms now?"

"Sure."

We walk through the swinging doors at the end of the corridor into the operating room. The drug cabinets are open and empty. Here is where they wheeled me, thumping my stretcher against the doors as we passed through. Alien smells—plastic, anesthesia, antiseptic—still hang in the air as if they will last forever.

In the main surgical suite we stop, looking up at the circle of fluorescents that once lit up the whole room. Flat on my back, zonked out of my mind, my little paper surgical hat covering my hair, I was transfixed by this chilling, man-made sun.

It all comes back with a wallop—the nurses' faces, the clink of instruments: "Are you Dorothea?" "Ba-boom, ba-boom, ba-boom"—the heart beating. "Oh, God. Oh, God. Oh, God."

Two days later we return to the hospital with cameras, tripod, lamps, tape recorder, and a notepad to record the final visit. A different guard greets us, an older man, busy eating a brown-bag lunch. "No, no other guard mentioned you would be coming," he snuffles as he eats. "Who said you could come in here?" I show him an old letter of permission from the hospital administrator and the director of public relations.

"No, see these letters don't mean nothing. I have to have permission from someone now at the hospital."

I have the urge to give his chair a swift kick and send him flying. I point out these letters *are* from someone at the hospital and tell him about our work with cancer patients, about needing to finish up before the contractors come in and tear the goddamn place apart.

"That's right," he nods his head happily. "The contractors are coming in on Friday."

"Right. That's why we have to get in here before . . ."

"Yup, nothing left here at all except a bed without a mattress and two chairs. Doctors came and took the lockers a week ago."

"Well, you can see we won't be stealing anything."

"What do you want to do in there, anyway? Take pictures? Pictures! Oh, no, see, that's different. This here hospital has regulations about pictures."

I call the public relations director, telling him how much I want to write about the closing of the old hospital and my memories of it as a former patient. No he says. "It's a real mess in there. You could get hurt."

Gene and I decide to sneak back into the hospital—we should have gone right in that first day. This should teach us once and for all to quit doing things the right way.

No guard at the front desk. We walk on through to the O.R. The huge overhead light mesmerizes me again. I feel, if I could just sit down here with my tape recorder, I would be able to remember the last two years. But Gene has no time for such notions. He is busy giving vent to his resentment toward the hospital administrators. He says, "Maybe they don't want me to take any pictures in here because they're afraid of what people will think."

"What are you talking about?"

His imagination is going into third gear now. "Look at all the equipment just left here—those operating lamps and stainless steel sinks. They probably got it all on government grants and, now that they have the new hospital, maybe they're going to sell all of this stuff—even though it might not be theirs to sell. Or maybe they don't want us extolling the virtues of this old place now that they've shut it down."

When I finally run into a guard, I am overjoyed he is the same young fellow who gave us pemission to come back. "Hi. I'm glad to see you. The other guard gave us such a hard time."

"Sorry," he says. Shaking his head. "The hospital called and said specifically, 'No pictures. Don't let anyone in, not even the Brookline police.'"

"Not even the police?"

"Oh, what's the point," I think. I am furious. Disgusted. And I am really tired, tired of closed doors. Eighteen months of closed doors. Administrators, doctors, social workers—as concerned with hiding their own shortcomings as with easing the cancer patients' burden. I am so sick of medical secrecies masking as rules and regulations. It seems I have come full circle. The writer who believed she had a heartwarming and urgent story to tell is still running into dead ends. The trusting romantic is a stupid romantic.

We walk outside around the high, yellow brick walls, past a dumpster and some barrels, marked "Do Not Remove." Well, at the very least, Gene can photograph me standing in front of the hospital.

Papers sift and blow in the light breeze, fluttering across the wide expanse of lawn. I pick some up. They are patients' records from 1967, 1977, 1979, 1980. Hospital admission records complete with physicians' diagnoses. Small, white index cards:

> Claire W—from Weymouth with cancer of the cervix,
> diagnosed in November of 1968 when she was 33.
> Cause of death and date: 1/74 alcoholism, cirrhosis of liver.
> Lillian W—age 43; cancer of breast, right.
> Luanne G—admitted 6/23/80; age 30; married; Catholic;
> admitting diagnosis: endometriosis; staff phys. Robert W. Kistner.
> Andrea G—admitted 7/8/80 at 12:42; age 27;
> admit. diag.: rt. lower quadrant pain.

I almost laugh at the irony of it all, but it's too painful. I remember the doctors and administrators who said they believed our work was a real violation of "patients' right to privacy."

A January 17, 1980, booking schedule for the O.R. lists the names of nine women who had abortions. Gene takes a picture of me holding the records. I am very angry. I suppose it will show in the set of my mouth, in my rigid hands.

Click, click, click goes Gene's camera. He stands me next to a decaying sign and exposes the whole roll of film. It is not much of a picture: the sign, the hospital, and me, unsmiling. The sign reads:

BOSTON HOSPITAL
O   WOM   N

Oh women, indeed!

Ten thirty at night and the wind is still knocking against the windows. All day it has been slamming against the house. I would call it a tumultuous wind but I imagine Gene shaking his head. "Much too dramatic," he would say.

Tonight should be Halloween. The leaves are last-gasp yellow; almost all of them are off the trees gusting mysteriously into the icy air, drifting across car headlights. The wind blows them against the curbs. Then, in the wake of passing cars, they blow back in swirling circles to the center of the street.

I think tonight of the long dead—surely he must be long dead—Fred E. Smith of Denmark, Maine, whose 1884 journal I bought last summer in the antique store at Adams Lake. Fred Smith intrigues me and angers me, too. What faithfulness or perserverance to write day after day in his diary—not every few months as I am doing now. But each of his entries is only four lines long, and he chooses to write mostly about the weather.

"Pleasant and warm. Commenced haying. Been down to L. H. Ingall's store this evening."

"Cold today. No snow. Went down under the hill tonight."

What does it mean to go down under the hill? When I am being fanciful, I imagine him going to some weird kind of rite held in the deep woods or in a cave under a hill in the wilderness.

Fred Smith never mentions parents, or wife, or children, although he does record the names of his relatives and friends who died during the year, making me believe he was not so young. Or, perhaps, he had been sick the way I was, and his mortality sat heavily on him, too. Terse as his descriptions are, they could be his way of making sense out of too quickly passing days, months, and years—not in poems or in a book, but in a way that had meaning to him.

To record "cold," or "warm," or "misty and rainy today," he must have seen the hoarfrost on the dawn grasses and the spiderwebs, like precious necklaces, beaded with moisture. Lucky Fred Smith.

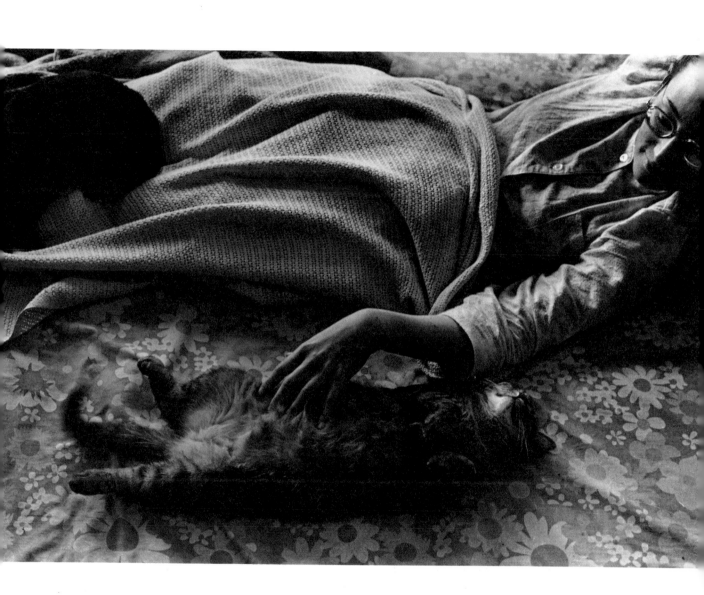

This morning I receive a letter, bursting with memories, from my old friend Cherie Anthes. So many times this holiday season I've thought of her still living with her husband in Arkansas, and still working as a county health nurse. Her letter, which I read and reread, is a journey back to revisit people who were our neighbors and friends in the delta: Corrinne McGowan, a blind woman who cared for two blind and retarded sons; the sexy, battered civil rights activist, Ezra Greer; Mrs. Brown, who chewed tobacco and told stories that turned the twentieth century landscape back into a slave plantation.

The older I get the more I realize it is these people, whose lives I have only touched tangentially, who have permanently shaped my consciousness. So, I am forever straining backwards, peering at them, wishing I had kept a better journal, taken more snapshots, kissed and hugged them a lot more. That's why it is so good to hear from Cherie. She is one of those people, one who is still accessible.

I imagine Cherie home from the clinic, tired, resting her feet up on the porch railing. Throughout the letter she inquires as to how I'm feeling, then adds a few lines about herself. "I'm reasonably happy" she insists, "though sometimes I'm a little confused and concerned about the future. Should I still be thinking of having children?"

When I write Cherie I will tell her I, too, am always wondering who I am, what I'm learning, and where I want to go. My questioning has to do with being thirty-seven, having cancer, being unmarried. Gene and I go on, many of our old problems resolved, others ongoing. He is staying part time this month in New York looking for jobs. Though he's associated now with a photo agency, his work is still out of the mainstream. His latest picture essays, about a prison and poor people, are said to be difficult on audiences. So he gets depressed, and sometimes he still retreats from me.

So there are splits in our life that I fight against, though I must admit the time away from him hasn't been wasted. I've read that to be creative can require a special environment. Incredibly, this has come to mean being alone to write, and to think my very own thoughts.

My life keeps turning around and around on me. Once I feared I might be living Emily Dickinson's poem. What is that line? "My life closed twice before its close . . ." Suddenly, I'm accelerating, rearranging priorities, studying my craft, writing more. I just mailed off an article about an extraordinary family of dwarfs to a magazine and I will drive out to Ohio next month to spend time with spiritualists who search the night skies for UFOs. At the end of December I'll join Gene in Denver to work on a story on emergency medicine.

Finally, with some confidence, I can say that I am a writer. A writer. Last week, editors of two magazines, one in San Francisco, another in Boston, telephoned to say I was doing fine work. I can't express how much this means to me.

I wait for Gene on a New York avenue, my day over, appointments made and met. People stream by the car window. The buildings rise around me, Pan Am to the north. From newstands in the thirties, from a vendor in Soho, from stores on the West Side, people are buying my magazine piece on the dwarfs, my very first cover story, and even now they are reading it. Oh, look at that sky. Day is done and the warm air is breaking up all over Manhattan. Snow dots the car window.

"I don't mean to block you in," says a man in a tan Datsun. "If you want to move your car I'll be in number 257."

Move the car? Move? I am so happy I'd rather dance.

SEVEN

I sit here crying and crying, unable to pull myself together. My eyes are swollen, and my mouth stings with salt. The second shoe has finally dropped. I found a swelling yesterday a lump on the same side where I had my mastectomy. An aspiration into two lymph glands shows malignant cells.

December 31, 1981

Cherie,

I had stopped my letter and am starting up two weeks later, two weeks that have turned my life upside down again. The day I was writing you, I found a lump on the same side where I had my mastectomy. So these past weeks have been full of grief, anger, fear, and thwarted plans. No Denver for Christmas. After an aspiration into my lymph glands (which are creating the swelling near my collarbone) showed malignant cells, I had a bone scan and blood work which happily showed no other metasteses. Radiation will begin probably the second week in January. This time though I will also be adding nutritional therapy, which the radiologists sort of sneer at—politely though—and I contemplate changing some of the focuses and stresses of my life. Once I thought cruel the suggestion that cancer patients have a lot to do with the ways in which their

bodies fail. Now, I am asking myself, are there ways that I am
contributing to the spread of the disease?

Sorry to lay some of this news on you, but truly, I have
recovered from the shock of it and am already setting up new plans
and well-plotted detours. Actually, the longer I have this disease,
the more I am learning about the happiest ways to live—with lots
of beloved, reliable friends and with better defined priorities and goals.
So don't feel bad for me. I have a strange and challenging life.

I would love to hear from you again, when you get the time. Happy
New Year.

Much love,
Dorrie

I have tried to approach this cancer cure through macrobiotic philosophy with an open mind, asking myself, sternly what do you really know about it? Don't be like your family and condemn things before you know what they're about. But it is a struggle.

Last week I had an appointment with a naturopathic physician, Ron Smith, but I want to get other viewpoints on natural healing before seeing him again. Until a week ago, my knowledge of macrobioticism came largely from conflicting news stories. "Beth Ann and Macrobioticism" detailed the self-starvation of a young girl by fanatic adherence to something called Diet Number 7. And a Dr. Sattilano wrote a personal account of his being "cured" of his prostate cancer through a radical change of diet.

I pay fifteen dollars to a well-dressed man for an afternoon session at the Kushi Institute. When I ask if he needs identification for my check, he laughs, "I never check the identification of a pretty girl." Everyone here seems to know one another, and there are many children wandering around. The woman sitting next to me, who had been manning the cash box earlier, is eating a date and nut bar. She answers my questions without hesitation.

"Oh yes, many people have registered for the weekend. Over sixty."

She unwraps another bar, licking her fingers. "Yes, many of them are cancer patients or their families. My father died of cancer."

Everything is running late; there is a half-hour wait before the next lecture "Self Diagnosis." Self diagnosis. I imagine generations of Harvard educated doctors cringing, even rolling over in their grave at such heresy. A middle-aged woman is sitting on one side of me, talking to a friend. I can hear a few words, "Cancer . . .

chemotherapy ... last resort." After the friend leaves, she reads from a book on macrobiotics, gasping in pain every few minutes. But no one pays attention to the sounds she makes. She goes on turning the pages.

"How is your wife?" someone asks a man who is going out the door. He looks like a Texas oil baron, golden cream silk suit over an obese body, a flash of gold chains at his throat and wrist.

"I just called her, and she said she's going to discontinue chemotherapy," he beams.

"Wonderful," chirps the woman munching her date and nut bar.

"Wonderful," echo voices throughout the room. "Isn't that wonderful?"

"Many factors affect our health, but two are of primary importance: the way we think and the way we eat ... The naturopathic physician believes that each person has an inherent ability to live in health, to recover from disease." As we drive from Boston to Connecticut, Gene reads aloud from a handbook on naturopathic medicine and writes down my new questions for the doctor. Can I eat eggs and cheese? Popcorn? Barley?

He waits for me in Dr. Smith's cheerless living room. The house is cold and bare, with little furniture and no pictures on the walls. No ornaments. I sit back on the examining table, a gynecologist's couch covered with waxy paper, but I can't relax. I do not like being examined by him. He makes mistakes, forgetting medicines I am now using or what he has allowed me to drink and eat. And I sense he does not like to touch me. He gingerly moves his fingers over the lumps near my collarbone but only glances at my swollen arm. The only time he shows any emotion is when I tell him the radiologist is confounded by the "good condition" of my irradiated skin. Then, he is pleased; his diet, of course, is the reason.

Ron Smith's skin is orange from carotene, his clothes a size too large. He offers me spiced apple tea, pointing out that his supper of yams and carrots is on the stove ready to be cooked. He says he wants me to think about coffee enemas, liver shots, the evils of meat, totally giving up white flour. He wants me to question whether or not what I eat and think is life promoting. He tells me this will be my last chance to get healthy.

After nightfall, Gene and I drive away through the Connecticut countryside, stopping, in an icy rain, at a motel called the King's Inn. Our room smells of old clothes, and the only decoration on the peeling walls is a red square of wood that once held a painting. The room clerk answers my phone call for bed coverings with a bunched-up blanket. "That's the dirtiest blanket I've ever seen," Gene laughs and drops it in a heap on the floor.

I sit on the bed next to Gene wearing my little teddy underwear, which shows off my thinner legs and hips. After Gene shuts off the lights, he puts his arm under my head, so I roll against him. He kisses me, his lips big and soft against mine. The bristles of his beard scrape against my throat. I feel my stomach flutter, and lower down, the insides of me open. It is always thrilling, always new, this response of mine.

May 5, 1982. I am trying to write my friend Louise. I have had another recurrence in the lymph nodes, which means January's radiation isn't going to take care of it after all. Of course, each time I have gotten tumors, I think I am dying. The surprise is that the doctors keep pulling me back from the edge.

On the plus side, I have planted my garden and am growing melons, carrots, cucumbers, lettuce, peas, marigolds, asters, anemones, and zinnias. It's nine-by-nineteen feet, and I turned it all by myself.

My handwriting isn't mine. I look at the black characters as they move slowly across the page and I can see the writing is not mine. It's terrifying. I am a character in one of Le Carré's spy novels, or a drug addict, or a schizophrenic who lives in a dozen worlds. But, of course, I am none of these things. What is happening is that the doctors are stealing my brain, bit by bit, and I am cooperating with them.

My handwriting isn't mine. I am thirty-eight, again a cancer patient. Four months ago in December of 1981, the cancer returned in my lymph nodes. They irradiated me, but in April, it was back again followed by headaches and weakness on one side of my body. Diagnosis: brain tumors which had to be treated before attacking the lymph nodes with chemotherapy.

So they slapped me down, got a CT scan to find the metastases, and zap—sixty seconds on one side with the linear accelerator, sixty seconds on the other. And, of course, I am taking something called Dexamethasone, which is a steroid.

But they make it sound so easy! Sure, you'll lose your hair like you did before with chemotherapy, but it is only ten radiation treatments to the head. It couldn't be simpler.

One of the best radiologists in the country, I am told, Dr. William Bloomer, is the man monitoring my case. He's brilliant, they say. I'm sure it is so. But no one at the outpatient clinic tells me that radiation burns. My tongue, nose, throat, and lungs feel that they have been scraped and salted. Sometimes in the car, I hold my mouth open out the window, letting the air cool the burn.

No one tells me the steroids will make me a space-cadet, wheeling around like a pinwheel, unable to pull a word from my head, to think a coherent thought. When I talk to my friends, I sound like a twelve-year-old, not able to say anything of consequence, yet they look at me as they always have.

Now, I am beginning chemotherapy, and this time around Gene and I have tried to ask the right questions. It isn't fair for a patient to have to watch such terrible things happen to his body without understanding they are going to happen. Methotrexate, one of the three chemotherapy drugs to be used, can damage the brain. But what a time to tell me—minutes before I am to receive the drug.

Buzz, buzz, buzz. I am the fly. The noise can't be stopped unless it is I who am stopped. Buzz, buzz. Between the little tumors in my head, the rest of my body, and the outside world, there is a barrier of chemicals. I am a fly in a bubble.

Steroids flow in little green pills to my brain, making my food taste awful, water sour. I move as if through molasses. Are there words for what I'm trying to communicate, I ask myself, tearing thoughts apart, puzzling, losing sense. I sound like an idiot. How can you sound so stupid?

Last night I woke up many times and thought of the garden I planted out back. I pictured it growing, filaments reaching, tendrils, hairy protuberances cracking through the soil. I lay awake in bed pulling up weeds, pulling them out like I pull out my own hair—rake and stir; lift it free. All night the windows glowed as if dawn were on the way, but it was ten o'clock, then two o'clock, then three o'clock.

I thought of the garden getting stronger, but it was not a benevolent image. The garden was breathing on its own.

Dr. Bloomer wishes me a quiet "good luck." He will not commit himself to cures, merely improvements, but I don't expect anything else from him. Still, he is less cold than he has been. We even talk about new wigs for my bald head.

Little Jennifer, the technician, kisses me and reaches up to put her arm over my shoulder and around my neck. "You have been," she says, "the kind of person who makes it all easier for us." But I honestly don't understand what she means. Can it be that the other patients who were with me each treatment day have been giving the techs a hard time? Or, perhaps, people have been responding to me all along as, God forbid, the archetypal "perfect patient," the steroid space-cadet, the smile.

I say good-bye to the pretty young girl who looks like she is on steroids too, smiling at all of us, and good-bye to the devastated woman with the unkempt hair who walks with a cane and wears a brace around her neck. When she moves we listen to her wheeze. "You have yourself a good summer," she says to me. "You do that."

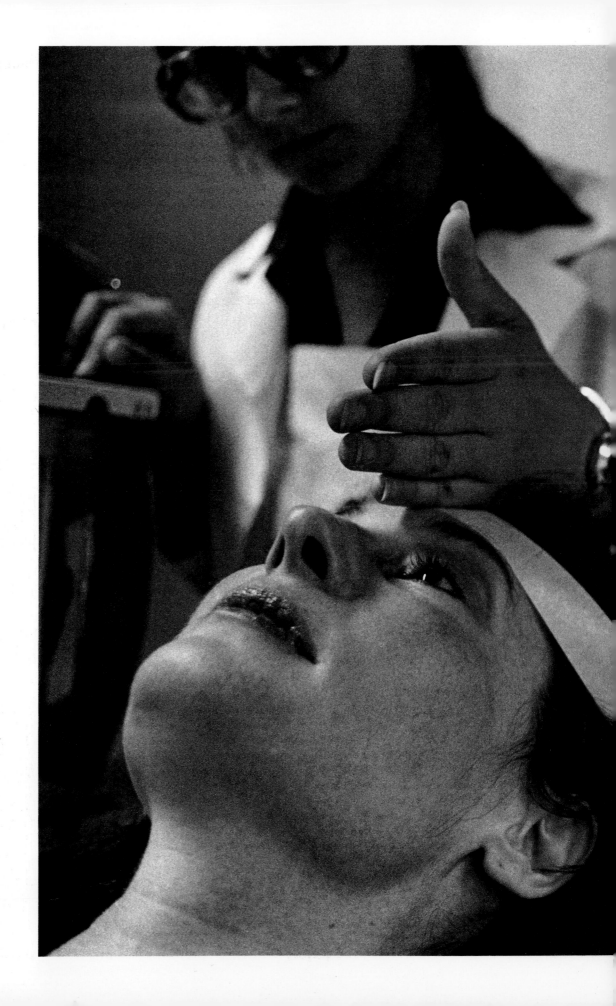

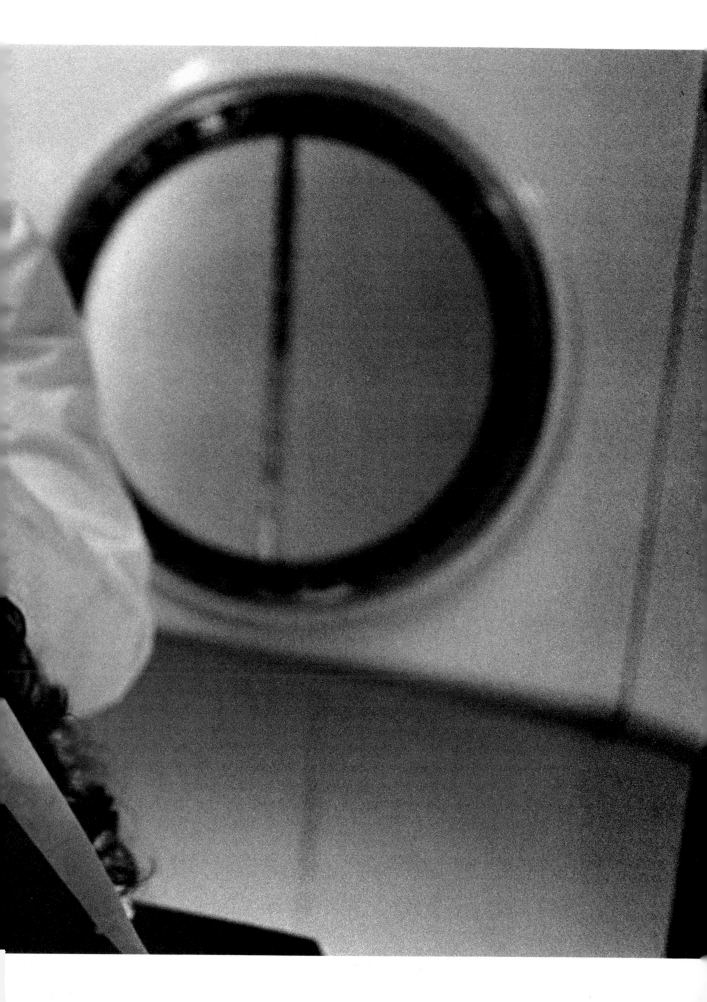

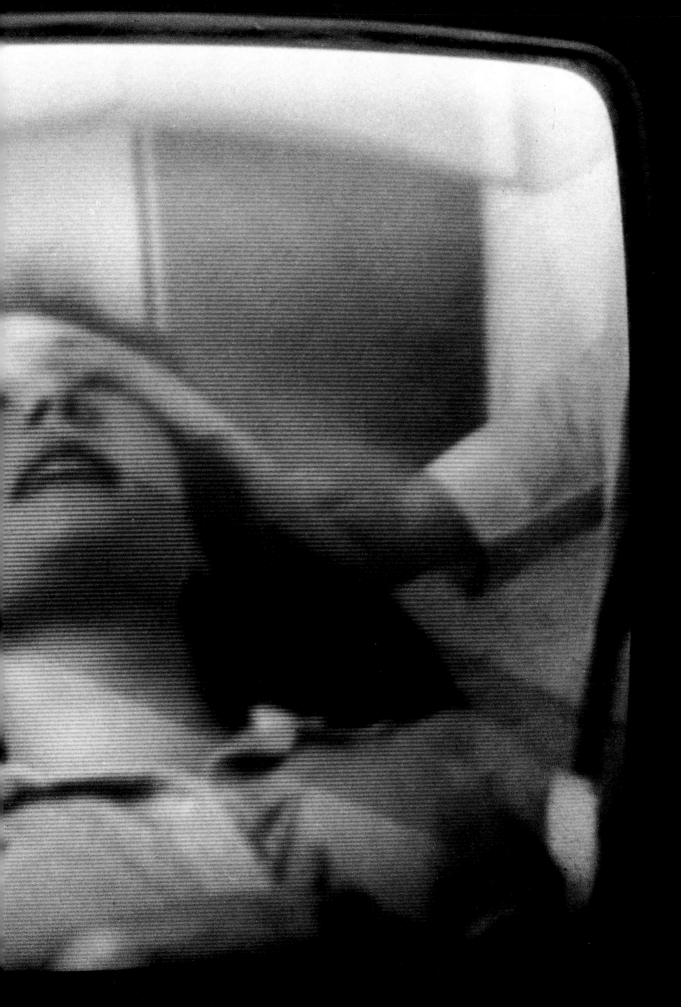

I will never forget her as long as I live, with her head thrown back as she hobbled away, hair in black straggles. "Far too long for a forty-year-old woman," my mother would have said. And along the back of her skull from top to bottom, a wide white scar like teeth in the grass.

Back in the hospital. Tonight, my first night with no fever, I am dreaming of Gene lying full length beside me, kissing him, and kissing him, and touching him. It is the first erotic dream I have had since the steroids began three months ago.

"Attention. This is a 'Code Blue' in 14 West . . . Please, this is a 'Code Blue' in 14 West."

I hear running feet. Someone down the hall is dying. I need to get up, to see for myself. Is she still fighting to stay alive? But I lie here, comfortable and warm, listening to one of the nurses trying to get through to the Mission Hill Church.

"We need a priest," she says, "and all I can get at that number is a recording."

A priest. Extreme unction, the oil on the eyes and on the feet. I was eight years old when I learned that, like everyone else, I, too, must die someday. Trembling, holding onto a girlfriend, I listened to the nuns at St. Mark's lecture on mortality and the last rites. The words "extreme unction" still hang in my memory like bells of doom. Darkness, holy oil, candles, and the priest anointing and praying, moving in a circle around the bed.

The nurses tell me that Mary, the Indian grandmother who came into the hospital in a beautiful gold-edged sari, has stabilized. Maybe her family, which has been waiting in the corridor for a week, can take her home to India. Eighteen seats have been reserved on an airplane.

A couple of days ago the family gave a present to the nursing staff, a picture of a boat and water and trees, worked in gold thread on a dark background. "It could be anywhere," I said. "This is where Mary's home is," the nurse told me. "This is where they are bringing her to die."

The steroids make me dream even when I am awake. It is always summer now in my dreams. I am an actress, very thin, and I have a new body, elegant in a gold dress. And my lover is of an age—a father figure. It is Jason Robards, and he is writing the play I am to act in.

At the theatre Jason directs me to ad lib the opening lines, something current from the news, to give my part relevancy. So when the curtain goes up, I stride out fearlessly onto the stage and say, "Do you know that the killing in El Salvador has been going on for some time?" The audience bursts into laughter—hilarious, mocking shrieks—until Jason comes onstage and asks them to be patient. He is going to rewrite those lines.

I stand facing the audience, unembarrassed, waiting for Jason to return. I grow tired. I slump. The audience begins to leave in little, nervous groups.

Hospital. Six o'clock in the morning. What you miss most is the fresh air. This is a tomb. We are sealed in, with all of us clamoring to get out, to breathe, to get better, or to get a stronger sleeping pill. What wakes you again and again are the voices, the footsteps, the heavy roll of the portable scale.

A doctor from Brigham and Women's Hospital is sticking a long, long needle into my neck. Zing-zing. After he freezes the area, he begins poking, pressing on my neck until I can hardly breathe. The nurse Karen takes my hand, and I squeeze hers. Oh, it is so scary, and it hurts. Another nurse takes her place, Marilyn, who grips my fingers until we sweat. Their eyes watch mine; sympathy, here's sympathy for you, and they nod from time to time. Finally the doctor puts a line in my superior vena cava, the big vein that leads into my heart. I wonder if he could miss or if my body will object to the sudden rush of medicine. They send in a tired x-ray technician to make sure everything is "properly placed."

Too many antibiotics. Too many confused thoughts. My ears ring when I get up to pee Monday night, ring and roar on Wednesday, roar like a seashell held to the ear with the sounds of the rest of the world barely filtering through.

Mystery, what a mystery this life is. The plants are filling out. The garden out back of our house sprouts one-half-inch here, an inch there, and I am changing too; cancer plods on from node to node, remarkable and not remarkable at all, like summer itself. Just another growing season after all. Is this resignation? I hope not. I do not intend to give up without a struggle, but more and more I see myself as a thread in a huge and royal tapestry—important to the central design but having an end, a place, a physical destination.

I think of the young daughter in Satyajit Ray's *Pather Panchali*, spinning, whirling in the rain, her hair flying out like a flag the night she died. I think of Sally Powers, who had just turned seventy. No one is special, are they, when all is said and done? And, of course, each of us is very special, very singular, carrying weight. I matter. Sally mattered. I would like to open the window tonight and yell that outside. I matter. Or go down and lie next to the plants and whisper it.

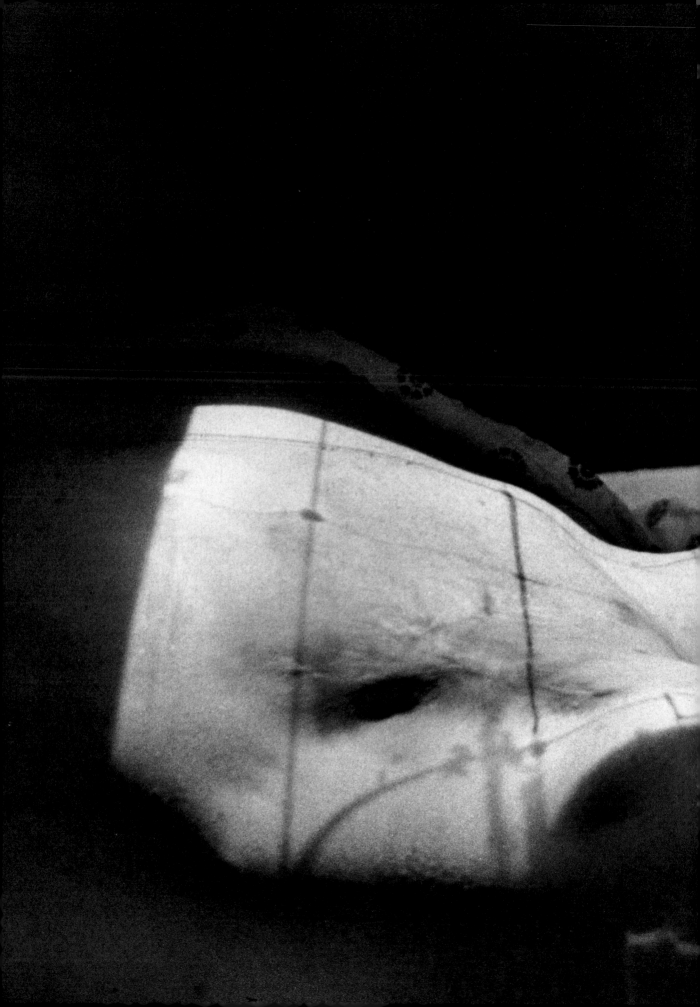

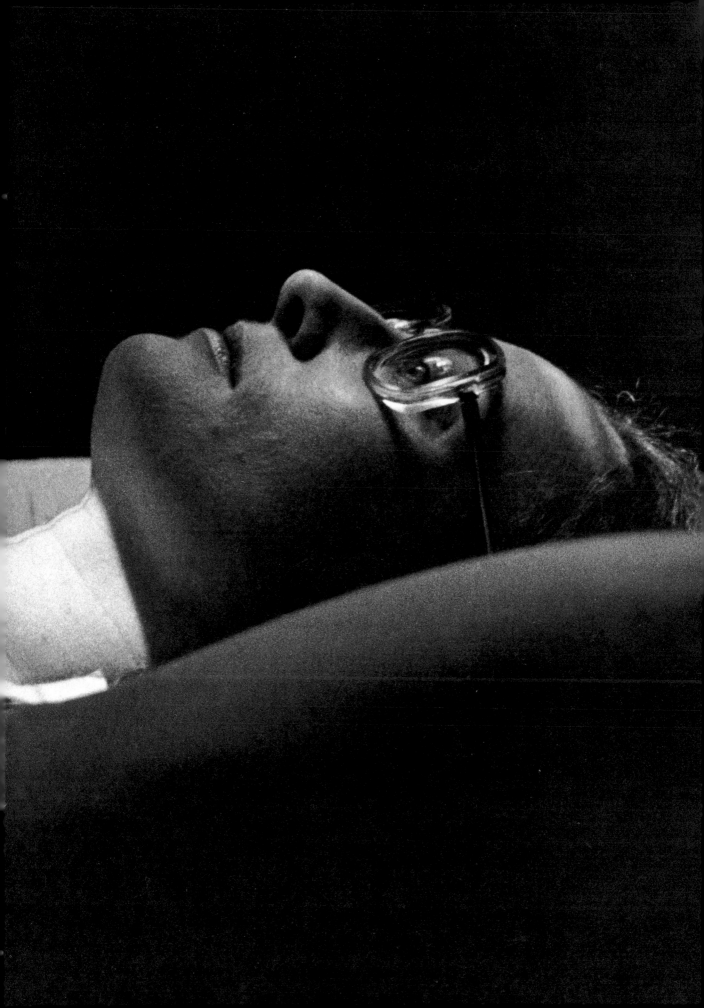

October 7, 1985

For almost two years I have been sleeping half on the floor or against
the wall, not wanting to move Dorothea's notebooks and diaries off my bed.
On hot, humid nights, pages, loose from their binding, stick to my back
and my shoulders; in winter, when I try to turn over, they
crackle like dried leaves. Still, I can't move them. Almost
everything else that belonged to her—clothes, car, jewelry—has
been donated to charity, sold, or carried off by friends.

Here it is, a hopeful October morning. I drink coffee and catch
the news on TV. At ten o'clock, I telephone the office, but there are
no messages, no assignments, no urgent need for me to do anything.
I wander back up to the bedroom and close the door. What's
outside blurs, recedes, and I am alone again with Dorothea.

I flip through the big, red diary and the ledger book in which
she wrote her dreams. Time swings back and forth—1975,
1983, 1979. Dorothea has thick, tangled brown hair; a cap of
prematurely gray hair; the babyish fuzz that grew in after her first
chemotherapy treatments. Lying on the bed, closing my eyes,
I begin seeing places and reliving experiences at the same time.
I see Dorothea kneeling in the garden laughing, pinching
a tiny, ripe tomato from its stalk; and the dark,
rainy streets outside Mt. Sinai Hospital. I see the old cemetery
at Adams Lake and the room in which Dorothea died.

Eugene Richards

FOR PHOTOGRAPHER HERMAN TELL 1938–1980

All rights reserved under International and Pan-American Copyright Conventions.
Published by the Aperture Foundation, Inc., in association with Many Voices Press.
Distributed in the United Kingdom and Europe by Phaidon Press Ltd., Oxford; in Italy by
Idea Books, Milan; and in Australia by George Allen & Unwin Australia Pty Ltd., North Sydney.

Exploding Into Life was prepared for Aperture by Eugene Richards and Carole Kismaric. The text was
edited from Dorothea Lynch's diaries, and the book designed by Eugene Richards. Carole
Kismaric was project editor.

Composition by David E. Seham Associates, Inc., Metuchen, New Jersey. Printed in laser-scan
duotone by South China Printing Co., Hong Kong.

Library of Congress Catalog Card Number: 85-70046
ISBN: 0-89381-177-7 cloth

As a courtesy, the names of certain individuals in Exploding Into Life have been changed.

Aperture Foundation, Inc., publishes a periodical, books, and portfolios of fine photography
to communicate with serious photographers and creative people everywhere. A complete catalog
is available upon request. Address: Aperture, 20 East 23 Street, New York, New York 10010.

A John Simon Guggenheim Memorial Foundation grant supported the early stages of this work; grants
from the National Endowment for the Arts and the Polaroid Corporation provided partial funding for
the publication, and additional support was forthcoming from Donald Dietz, Elizabeth Hamlin, Marnie
Samuelson, John Samuelson, and Harry Mattison.

I wish to thank Carole Kismaric; Harry Mattison; Wendy Byrne; Elizabeth Hamlin; Fred Ritchin; Charles
Mikolaycak; Janine Altongy; Tom Fitzgerald; Susan Backman; the staff of Boston's Photographic Resource
Center; and my parents, Helen and Gene, for their precious guidance and understanding. -E.R.